2014

OFFENSIVE LINE COACHES HANDBOOK

FEATURING LECTURES FROM THE 2014 C.O.O.L. CLINIC

Edited by Earl Browning

COACHES CHOICE™

www.coacheschoice.com

ISBN: 978-1-60679-312-1

ISSN: 1945-1172

Telecoach, Inc. Transcription: Emmerson Browning, Kent Browning, and Tom Cheaney

Diagrams: Cheery Sugabo

Book layout: Cheery Sugabo

Cover design: Cheery Sugabo

Front cover photo: Steven Bisig—USA TODAY Sports

Back cover photo: © Tom "Mo" Moschella/Icon SMI/ZUMA Press

Special thanks to John Widecan of the University of Cincinnati for taping the lectures.

Coaches Choice
P.O. Box 1828
Monterey, CA 93942
www.coacheschoice.com

Contents

CONDUCTING THE OFFENSIVE LINE: COMMUNICATION AND TEAMWORK

Cincinnati Bengals

Before we get started, I have three of our guys that I want to introduce. Russell Bodine, stand up. He is our new center from the University of North Carolina. He is a big, strong guy that is going to play center. We have Dan France from Michigan State University. He is a left guard. You saw him on film yesterday when Coach Mark Staten gave his lecture. Next we have Curtis Feigt from the University of West Virginia. He is originally from Germany. That is fascinating to me. He is also a good player. They are here to learn football.

Their job here is to think like coaches. They are here to learn football and to learn more than to just do their assignment. They are here to think like a coach would think. When they are done, they should be able to coach football if I have done my job and if they have done their job.

For those of you that have heard me talk before, I want to make you think. I am going to throw stuff at you, and I am going to give a perspective of different things. They may be a little off at times. I am not going to draw up football plays for you. I want to make you think so you can apply things to your own football situation.

There may be a lot of the pass protection drills on the video I am using. If you do not know my pass protection, particularly with the hands, I am not going to go back and teach it all. I am going to do a continuation from where we were last year and to what I have learned this year and to expand the different things we do in pass protection. I may be different than anyone in the profession on this subject.

An old man told his grandson, "My son, there is a battle between two wolves inside us all.

"One is Evil. It is anger, jealousy, greed, resentment, inferiority, lies, and ego.

"The other is Good. It is joy, peace, love, hope, humility, kindness, empathy, and truth."

The boy thought about it and asked, "Grandfather, which wolf wins?"

The old man replied quietly, "The one you feed."

The title of my lecture is: "Conducting the Offensive Line: Communication Teamwork." I had a bucket-list moment two weeks ago. I conducted the Hamilton-Fairfield Symphony Orchestra. That was crazy! It was a rush. I kind of worked on it for a year. I learned how to do this and prepared for it to happen. It was fun, but there were things I learned from that experience that have helped in my teaching. I am going to talk about some of those parallels as we go through this lecture.

We are going to knock the lights down low as everything is going to video here. (Photo—Paul conducting the Hamilton-Fairfield Symphony Orchestra) A person in an orchestra told me the members of the orchestra will be able to tell within 30 seconds if they are going to play with the conductor, or if they are going to play on their own and make the conductor follow them. I thought that was fascinating. Thank goodness that did not happen to me when I conducted the Hamilton-Fairfield Symphony Orchestra. I kind of thought of it as an NFL coach.

(Photo—Shark going after a person in deep water) This to me is like a young NFL coach with the shark potentially coming to devour you. The shark represents your own players. Your own players are your enemy, more than the players on the other team. I like to tell them that.

One thing I have a sense for NFL coaches is this: If you come into the NFL and know what you are talking about, and you can help the players become better, they are the easiest people in the world to coach.

On the other hand, if you come into the NFL and try to fake your way through the teaching, and you say something you do not know the right answer to, they will devour you like a piece of meat in the water. That happens. I want to encourage coaches, particularly young coaches, if you do not know something, say you do not know the answer to the player. You will learn the answer and know it the next time it is asked.

More important than anything else: be so good at what you do that you can help your players. No matter what your personality is, they will respond to you if you are able to do that.

How many of you have seen the TV show *Breaking Bad*? (Film—Clip of a conversation from *Breaking Bad*) I love it! Isn't that beautiful? Hey Bodine, he is my new center. Stand up! That is how I want you to be. Do you have it? When you make a call, and you change the blocking for someone else, that is what the other person will look like. Do you have it? You must be so convincing and so determined that there is no question that you are right. Do you have it? That was for you, Bodine.

So we are talking about the presence of the center. The center must have that type of personality. I really do not care if your center has this talent or that talent. If your center does not have that personality type of convincing determination, he will not be successful. Bodine has it, or we would not have drafted him. Your center must have that personality to be successful. We had a great center in Kyle Cook for a long time. He was just beat up. He was one of the smartest players I have ever coached.

This is probably the number-one trait I look for in a center. Can he lead? Can he think quickly? If he can block, that is a bonus, I guess. So I watch it just like that. Do you have it, Bodine? Bodine, do you have it? Alright! (Film—Clip from *Breaking Bad*):

"Say my name!"

"Heisenberg!"

"You're damn right!"

I love that scene. So there you go.

WAY TOO EARLY

Players that take off on the snap count too early end up on the tackle. "The defender beat me on the snap count. He was offside. They should have thrown a flag, but they didn't. He ran around and sacked the quarterback."

The tackle could not block that defender. What do you do? We run drills on how to block a defender that beat the blocker off the snap count. We practice that block. Because in your normal protection for a tackle, you take a nice three-step kick slide, and there you go. What you need to train the blockers to do is to feel their balance in their feet so if the defender takes off early, all you need to do is to pivot and go push on the rusher.

If you can rehearse it in the back of your mind, it will help. Think of plays where the linemen got beat off the count. Invaluable what the tackle did, because he is so ingrained in taking the kick step, he kicks, and then stands up. Then, his foot comes straight down in place. Then, he turns and chases the defender, and he is beat. I have seen this a million times in films. Let's take a look at some film clips.

We want the tackle to open and to push. We want to open and extend. When a defender has beaten you off the count, you know the techniques the rusher has used. He is going to come upfield and come around on you. So instead of kicking, you just turn and then push the rusher if he beats you off the count.

I have three shots of the techniques we use. These are the only three film clips that Brian Braswell, my new assistant, could find. He found these three film clips for us. He is an outstanding individual. He is from Morehouse College in Atlanta. He was the line coach there last year. The person that was in his job last time is now a running backs coach. His name is Kyle Caskey. The guy before that was Bob Surace, and now he is the head coach at Princeton.

What happens in one of the film clips, which I really hate more than anything, is that our back, without telling the tackle, thought the tackle was in trouble, and he just decided to chip the defender. Our tackle had the man blocked. He was pushing on the defender and he was in good position. As a general principle, I hate chip blocks. I despise chips. We do not do chip blocking unless the offensive coordinator makes us do them. I would never chip block.

I like it when our tight end gets upfield and hits the defensive back first. I like that move. But, in my opinion, the last thing the blocker wants is an unpredictable move by the rusher. When the good defenders see the back coming at him, we will make moves off the chip block.

When I first came into the league, chips were very effective. But they have gotten to the point that the defenders make moves when they see the back coming at them. As much as possible, we want that rusher to come at us predictably, where we know what he is going to do.

The drill is as follows. The defender beats him off the count, and the blocker turns and pushes the rusher (Diagram #1). The blocker wants to catch the rusher in his crossover step. You have to know as a blocker when you feel the rusher starts to cross his legs. You want to use his momentum against him as possible.

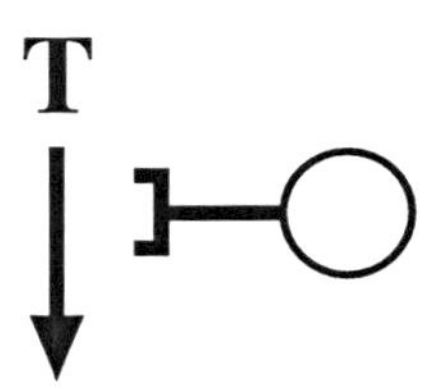

Diagram #1. Defender Beats Blocker on Snap Count

So much is involved when we block a defender and he hits the inside move, and he has not brought that backside leg through. You can feel the back leg weight transfer. and when it starts to happen, you want to push on the defender.

It is the same theory if you are blocking and you cross your feet and the defender hits you. That is not a good situation to be in. Blockers need to learn the point when the defender starts to cross his feet. When that happens, that is when you accelerate and finish the defender. We did drills on that issue this week and will do more next week on how you feel that move and when you make the push on the defender.

BLIND SCREEN AUDITION

This is a fascinating point. Music people started doing this about 25 years ago. When people audition for an orchestra, they now play behind a blind screen. If you saw a professional orchestra 50 years ago, it would be over 90 percent of Caucasian males. All white males! The reason for this is the fact they had their audition in front of people, and for different reasons that is whom they picked for the orchestra.

Today, if you look at a professional orchestra, it is much different than those demographics. Right! Today, the people that audition for an orchestra do it behind a screen.

Now, where does that go? A lot of times you put individuals together in groups to see how they sound and how they play together to make a decision. Many people can play as a soloist, but do not play well in a group without drowning out the other performers.

Why does this have anything to do with what we are talking about? One of the favorite sayings by Coach Marvin Lewis is this: "We all have to sing from the same hymnal." We all have to be on the same page effectively. We have to play as one.

If you listen to modern pop music, it is always with a consistent beat. The way they record modern music is with a "clicker." It is a sound that is played in the headphones of the person recording the music. It may be a guitarist, a singer, or with a track, but they all stay together. Then they put all of the tracks together. They all stay together with this technique.

Or they do it with a flashing red light that is on the wall. It is different if it was modern concert music, or if it was old music. By doing it this way, the music can be played fast or it can be played slow.

In music, shifting from playing fast or playing slow is called rubato. It means to rob. You may speed up somewhere, but you make up for that time frame by slowing the music down at another time frame. Over that time length, you have a consistent rhythm.

(Photo—Paul conducting the Hamilton Fairfield Symphony Orchestra) Here I was. The key is this: I had these 40 instruments, and we could have all stayed together. But that is not really music. You can do that with a clicker. The key was to get them to slow down and to speed up. To slow down, and to speed up, is the way to play good music. I am going to play 30 seconds of the music so you can hear what I am talking about so I can get to my next topic.

Here we are. I am conducting the orchestra. Now the beat is slow. Now it is picking up, and now it is going to slow down again. And the key is to get them all to play together as one. See how slow it is going now? It will slow down even way more than what it is now. I kind of loved the expressions on the faces of the musicians because they really enjoyed playing that way. It was so different from what you think of as popular music or anything you know today.

Now, why do I do all of this? I do it because it is important for our offensive line. For those that know me, you know I like to give some weird examples so I can make my point. Here is my point: You have to play as *one!* Our offensive line must play as one. Our new offensive linemen will have to do the same techniques that we use. As I get to know the new players, we are going to adjust the players' techniques a little to make what is more conducive for his body type. We will adjust to the players talents.

So in the run game, the footwork for every player has to be the same. Otherwise, you get players out of sync and off levels. You must play together.

- Blocking angles: run game footwork
- Calls are a contract
- Pass levels: consistent sets
- Jumping coordinated

When a center makes a call, he is making a contract with the players next to him. If I make a call where I say, "Middle," and in that case it means I am going to end up in the geometric middle of the two defensive tackles, I am going to stay in the geometric middle of the protection.

A center can never make a middle call and then when he feels there is nothing to do, he goes over to "kill" someone on the other side. The guard next to the center on the other side has lost confidence in the center because the center has broken his contract. He did not stay where he said he would stay.

If you have a slide call made by the center and he starts out to slide to the left, and I am not saying he will not twist back over to the side, but if he sees the left area is okay and he decides to slide over to his right, he cannot do that because that is a breach in his contract. His contract on the slide call is to stay on the side he called. That is so the players on his right side know what they have to do. The blocker on the left side knows the center is going to be there.

So commando blocking, I hate. I have a hard time with this. In a film, I will see one player jump his man, and another man do this, and another blocker do that. Good pass protection happens when everyone is in system levels.

When you have a jump, it is coordinated. It is tied in with the calls. You know exactly when that man is jumping. The call has to say, "Okay, tackle, on this call, you may jump. We do not have a call where the rule states: "Jump if you want." That does not happen. "On this call, you jump." It is center you jump. Guard, you jump.

We have multiple techniques we teach them. But I think it is important for it to be all coordinated and tied in with calls so the blockers know the levels they can work on. They need to know how they can handle games, and the like.

HIP-TO-HIP TIMING (WITH A BAG)

I have shown this drill before. We place a bag between two blockers, and they work on getting hip-to-hip on a square vertical double-team block (Diagram #2). We place a shield dummy or a dummy

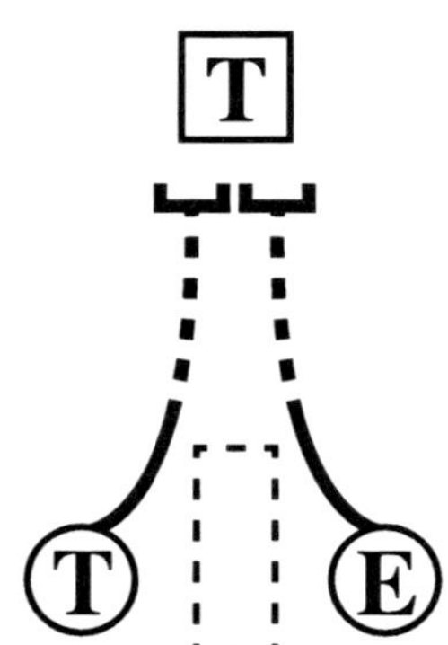

Diagram #2. Double-Team Drill—Hip-to-Hip Timing: Bag Between Blockers

pad between the inside hips of the two blockers. We want them to keep their hips parallel as they drive the defender back.

One of the big problems with the hip-to-hip double-team block is that we get one blocker in front of the other blocker. On the double-team block, the inside blocker (and you may want to call him the post blocker), his rule is this: He may not leave the defender until the blocker next to him gets hip-to-hip and they drive the defender off the line together.

If the defender does a swim move to the outside, the tackle has to chop his feet and hold his ground until he feels that he and the tight end are together. It is not a big deal if the defender we are double-teaming goes another way, because the tackle can go up to block on the linebacker. No! If his man goes away, he is to remain in his position until he feels a push and contact by the tight end. Otherwise, he gets soloed, and they get split.

The coach may have to hold the bag between the two blockers to start the drill. We are using the bag in the drill against a defender with a blocking dummy. After the snap count, the coach lets the bag go.

Following are a couple of points to consider when you double-team block. Don't let the blockers flare their elbows. The bag will prevent them from flaring their elbows. There is nothing worse than having two blockers getting vertical on a defender on the double-team block and the blockers are swinging their elbows and end up hitting their double-team buddy.

When you do the double-team block, keep your elbow in, keep the hands down, and have the inside hand come up together. Otherwise, you bang each other off the block.

This view is without the bag. This is what a double-team block should look like. It looks like a hip-to-hip vertical double-team block.

LINE CALLS

Let's talk about calls. Part of my lecture is about communication. Line calls should be short, crisp, and ideally they should be short and one single syllable.

I got this theory from a naval training officer. (Photo—Naval officer on the deck of a ship in battle) I have a prize for anyone that can tell me who the person in the photo is? Who? Woody Hayes! Yes, it is Woody Hayes. How about that? He used to tell his team these things that were passed on through Woody Hayes to Bo Schembechler, and then passed on to me about line play when I was at Michigan with Bo.

The line calls should be crisp calls and they should be short, single-syllable, and they should be guttural consonants. "Kisch" would have been a good line call. It is something that is sharp and crisp and can carry the sound. The calls should be inspiring. There should be a confidence to the call. They should be inspiring.

Bodine, when you make calls, I do not want to hear *tough* in a soft tone of voice. I want to hear tough in a tone of voice so you convince the blocker next to you that he is going to work!

Next are the pommel drills. These are some new drills I am doing with pass protection. For those of you that know what I do with the hand drills, I think you will like this. The guys that do not know what we do with our hand drills will be completely confused.

I do want to pass this along to you. We hire a service that grades every football player in the NFL on every play on film. Based on the information they receive, they give the players grades, and that helps us deciding on free agents, and it helps us with an objective opinion of our players. I use it as information when I watch opponents. The service charts the players' best moves, if they are playing at home or away, and a lot of different things which is interesting. Following is the chart they gave us.

Last Five Years (2009–2013)

1.	Cincinnati Bengals	80%
2.	New York Jets	78%
3.	Seattle Seahawks	77%
4.	Baltimore Ravens	77%
5.	Buffalo Bills	77%

The chart tells us we are ranked #1 in the NFL in offensive pass protection for the last five years. So some of the things we do with our hands, I kind of like it, you know?

Following is a second chart we received. It shows the rankings for the fewest hits on the quarterback from the blocking of the offensive line.

FEWEST QUARTERBACK HITS (OFFENSIVE LINE ONLY)

Bengals Rank (Last 5 Years)

2013: #1

2012: #1

2011: #1

2010: #19

2009: #2

Last 5 Years Average: Bengals #1

A lot of people may disagree on what I teach our players to do with their hands in pass protection. I am just here to tell you what I do, and I believe in what we teach.

Where is Jeffrey Barnett? Jeffrey Barnett is a coach from Guyer High School in Denton, Texas—4A State Champs in 2013 and 2014. Stand up, Jeff! His buddy is Kyle Keese. Kyle told me that Jeffrey does all of my stuff. Okay! He won two state championships. I bring this up for this point. Some of you may be saying, "I am a high school coach, and I am not able to teach the things Coach Alexander teaches because it is too hard." No! That is not true. Jeff has proven you can teach what we do with our hands.

POMMEL DRILLS

Keep Coming to Club

I teach the club move. It is as I said before: you need to know my stuff. When a defender comes outside we use a club move to make an attempt to club him. We grab the defender on most everything we do. We seldom punch. I use more martial arts, wrestling techniques as my basic techniques. We use this rather than using boxing techniques.

This is a drill that will help you. Some of the players that use our techniques will grab the defender's inside arm when he is wide outside. Your body has to move over in front of the defender. You throw your body out in front of the defender so you can cover him, and then hook him with the outside arm.

As the blocker comes across the line of scrimmage, the blocker may want to use the term "one more kick," which is great. The term I use is: "keep coming" (Diagram #3). The blocker must throw his body almost two feet to get in front of the defender.

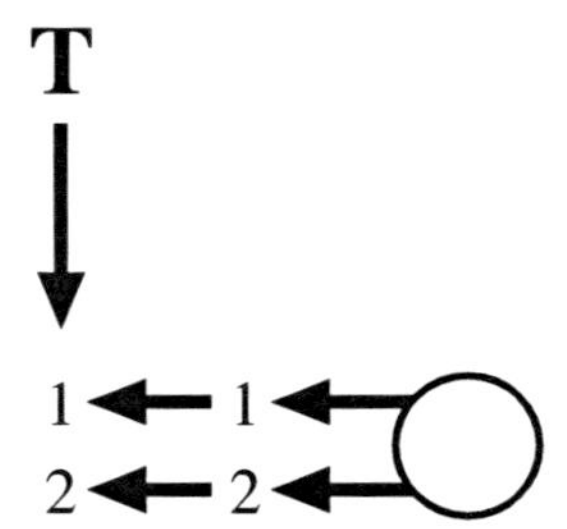

SLIDE MOVES

Diagram #3. Keep Coming

The blocker wants his body all the way in front of the defender so you can control him with your whole body. We want to use the "keep coming" technique on the club move.

LIFT VS. A RIP

Next is a "lift" versus a "rip" move, which is a timing move on the crossover. Think of it this way. It is this simple. When defenders rush inside, the goal of that defender is to break down the inside hand. If he can break down the inside hand, he will be able to beat the blocker inside.

There are only two ways he can break the blocker's inside hand down. The first way is for him to do a rip move, where he brings the offside arm through the blockers outside arm. As he does that move, he keeps coming all the way through. He is using his power by lifting his arm up as he comes through the blocker.

When he does the rip to the inside arm, look what happens to his back leg? It crosses over. It has to cross over.

The other way the blocker can break down the defender's arm is to take either hand to knock down his inside arm to continue through. So we use the "knock down, continue through, and feet/crossover."

Those of you that know me know one of my principles: We never punch an inside move. When a defender makes an inside move, the blocker should drop his inside hand. That is what I teach. Drop your inside hand because I go feet before hand.

I drop my inside hand as the defender starts to rip through. As the defender starts his rip move, the blocker takes his inside arm and places it on the top of the defender's inside shoulder pad. As the defender continues on his rip move, the blocker comes around the neck and shoulders of the defender.

This is the move we can use on the rip or the inside knockdown technique. The slogan we used last year was this: "Block him like a top." Use angular momentum to stop the charge of the defender (Diagram #4). Don't try to put your body in front of a force when you can deflect a force. It is much like what Blaise Winter was talking about last night. When the crossover begins, you accelerate your hands and feet.

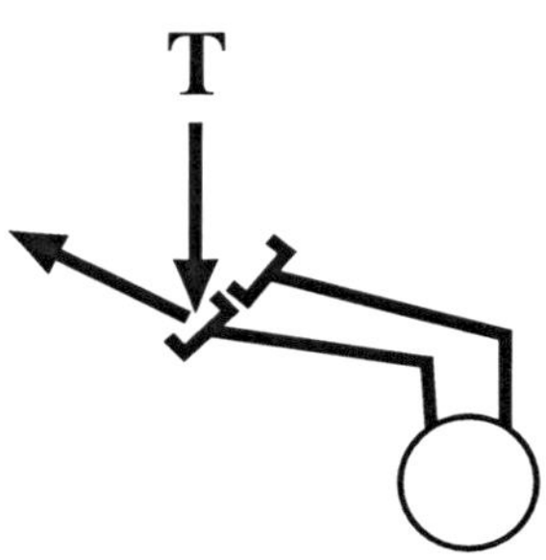

Diagram #4. Rip With a Crossover

ONLY ONE BASS IN THE ORCHESTRA

There is only one bass in the orchestra. I am talking about the big, fat musical instrument that you have to stand straight up when you play it. That is not really true, but no one really knows the difference. I know this: there is only one piccolo in the orchestra. This is because their pitch is so high. Usually, there are very few bass instruments in the orchestra because their pitch is so low. What happens is this. The middle sounds get drowned out because of the differences of the frequencies and the pitches.

In my first year in the NFL, coaching with the New York Jets, we were playing the Denver Broncos. John Elway was the quarterback for the Broncos. It was late in the fourth quarter, and we were ahead. Our fans were going wild. Denver was really good at that time. We were getting ready to beat John Elway and Denver. The crowd was going crazy, and everyone was cheering. The noise in the stadium was deafening.

The only thing I could hear was something from the line of scrimmage. "Set, Blue 88!" The only noise I could hear was John Elway calling the signals out on the field. It took me a long time to figure that situation out. I thought he must have had the loudest voice I had ever heard in my life. Finally, it donned on me why I could hear him. It was because his voice was down low. Your voice can project in those low frequencies, while all of the other middle-range frequencies are competing against each other.

When our center goes to the line of scrimmage, Bodine is not going to say, "Mike 5-2." He is going to say, "Mike 5-2! Mike 5-2!" He is going to repeat that call more than once. The call is going to be in a voice down where the other players can hear him. We could have him call out, "Mike 5-2" with a squeaky voice. We prefer not to operate that way.

It is like your mother. My wife is a master. She sits in the living room and bounces her voice off the wall to the celling and off the other wall across the room. She can hear her voice. I do not know how she can hear it. That is something women have on us. As we get older, our hearing is not as good. We lose our hearing. What is that comment? "It is God's gift to the married man." Very good, ha ha.

HE'S RUSHING OR HE'S NOT

If you are the guard, it is this simple. This is what we hear from the players: "Coach, I cannot tell when my guy is rushing, or if he is running a twist stunt. I could not read the loop man. Help me out."

Following is the theory that all blockers should know: He is either rushing you, or he is not rushing you. It is that simple. Don't think about a twist. He is rushing you, or he is not. If he is not rushing you with full speed, get back. Set levels with the man next to you. You do this so if it is a twist, you can pass the defender off.

We do not want our blockers working against a defender that is giving a half-ass rush, stand there at the line of scrimmage and think, "Oh gee, I have this defender beat." The next thing he knows, he is getting hit and gets picked on a game or stunt. So he is rushing you, or he is not rushing you. If he is not rushing you, it means the blocker is leveling. That is all you can do.

HE'S RUSHING YOU, OR HE'S RUSHING THE GAP

Sometimes, a guard, or it could be a center, tackle, or a tight end, you cannot tell if the defender on you is the drive man on the twist or not. The theory on that is simple. When you see a rusher you need to know if he is rushing you, or if he is rushing the gap. If he is rushing the gap, you flatten him and try to force it into a game, no matter what. He cannot be an effective drive man if he is rushing you. So when we watch the film and we see a twist, I ask this question: Is he rushing you, or is he rushing the gap? By doing so, they get a good read of what he is facing.

SHUCKING DRILLS

Don't get "stuck" (or grabbed) by an edge rusher. Those of you that know me know we have one rule for protection for the guards in particular. It applies to the center as well. The number-one rule is this: Don't get stuck on an outside rusher. If the defender rushes out, knock him outside to keep him off you. You do not want to be grabbed by the defender. If the defense does a twist, and he grabs the guard, you get beat. You can't just tell the coach, "They grabbed the guard." That is not a good enough answer.

If the defender rushes out, get him off of you. Get him off. Do it by deflecting his momentum with a block and a shuck. I have shown that technique a million times at this clinic. I will review the shuck so you can see what we are doing. This is what a left guard would do if the 3-technique defender rushes him to the outside (Diagram #5). He knocks him outside

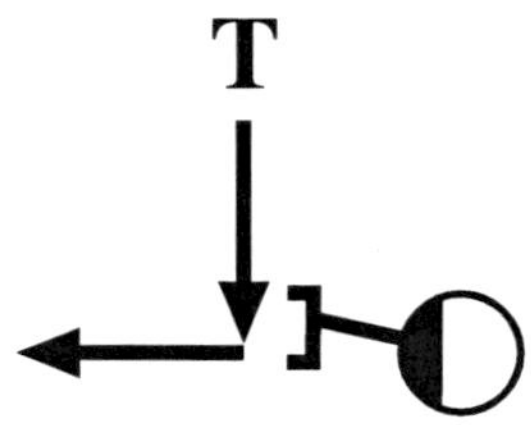

Diagram #5. Shuck Defender Outside

with a block and a shuck, no matter what. If it is not a game, then no harm, no foul. He would reset and block him again. Right! It is a block with the outside hand, and sidearm launch with the inside hand.

Next, we look at the shuck by the tight end. This is against a tight end twist (Diagram #6). This is a block with the left hand and a launch with the right hand.

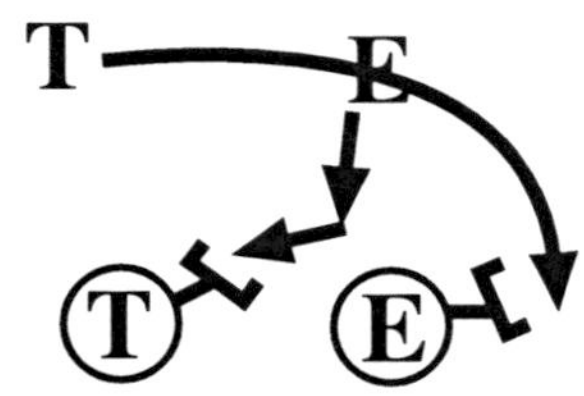

Diagram #6. Shuck Block by Tight End

Let's look at some of these drills. We line up three men in a triangle. I finally found a drill where we could use a basketball (Diagram #7). We did not want to use a medicine ball because I did not want them fighting the ball. I want them feeling the shuck as they let the ball go, and to keep their feet moving at the same time.

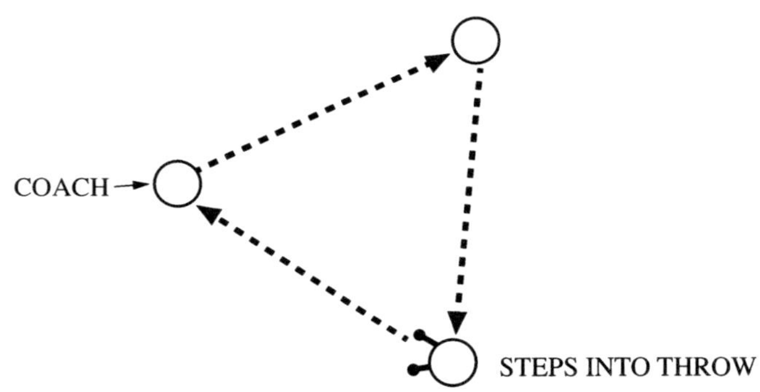

Diagram #7. Basketball Shucks

When you shuck a defender, you keep your shoulders square. You get back to your position after you make the shuck and set your feet in case the other defender is coming around on a twist move. This is a good drill because he is working his feet and his hands.

A person who knows how to block in pass protection really knows how to gather his feet. The move is much like you would use in throwing the shot put. It would be the glide part in the shot put.

Next, we look at the one-hand ball shuck (Diagram #8). We have Andrew Whitworth doing one-hand ball shucks. The thing he does that we like is that he gathers and moves his feet, and then lets the ball go with the outside arm. This is how you want them to launch a defender in a game.

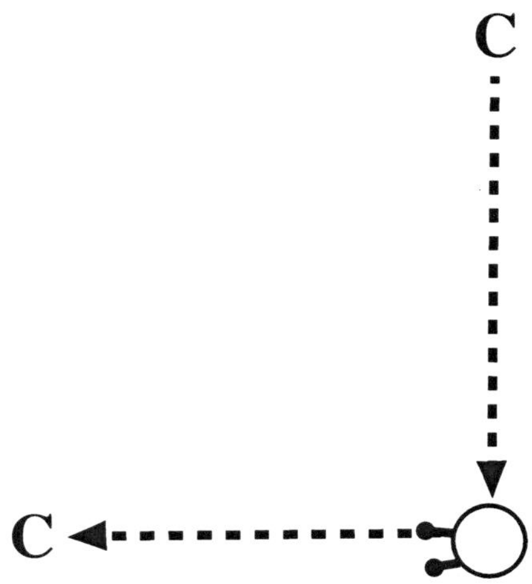

Diagram #8. One-Hand Ball Shucks

ARCHING, NOT SQUATTING

So many of the centers I see from college, and I see some high school centers at times, and the stances they are in remind me of frogs. They have their butts down low. I am talking about when the quarterback is under the center.

Ask Bodine what I asked him when I went down to North Carolina to work him out, and he got down in his frog stance. What did I say? Yes! I said, that stance will not work in the NFL. There is no way. After we got him back in Cincinnati, and were working out, I complimented him on his stance. He had changed his stance.

I learned this from Jim Sweeney, the former center for the New York Jets. He was a great center over 20 years ago. He told me where he got messed up on pass protection was when he started to sit back on his heels and to get his butt down.

In reality, the center wants to play with the legs extended as they can be, where you can move, but still have power in your stance. If you are a center that can only stay in your stance for 10 seconds before getting tired, then your stance is screwed up. The analogy to be coiled like a spring or like a cat ready to explode is no good. The most important thing is for you to be able to slide and to move your feet. You need to lower your knees, and you need to bend the knees. You are lowering your center of gravity.

THE BRILLIANCE OF SIMPLICITY

In math, if we have a hard equation and we need to do some function to it, the first step is to reduce the problem to its simplest form.

I like to talk about simplicity. I am talking about calls and rules for football. We have heard of coaches making things as simple as they can.

There is no brilliance in confusion. Don't make things like this. (Film—Clip from an old movie, showing the switching of the wine goblet trick. The villain thinks he is outsmarting the hero but he actually switches his wine goblet for the wine goblet with the poison in it. He drinks the wine and dies.)

CENTER-DIRECTED CALLS

There has to be a simple way to do this football thing. We are talking about calls and putting schemes together. Following are a couple of thoughts on this topic.

A Simple System For Blocking Rules

- The best tight ends are mute. Tight ends that like to make calls can screw things up more than anything going.
- The calls start from the inside to the outside. The center makes the call. The call gets passed to the outside so that everyone is blocked. So that you do not have it going all spread out.

When I coached in college, we used to have frontside and backside calls. No! Not now. I am at the point where we want the center to make the call, and then everyone plays off that call. It may be that the center identifies the Mike linebacker, or he may identify a person. The calls are very simple. If we do the counting, we can figure it out. The rookies have not figured it out yet.

If you go to Glazierclinics.com, there is a one-hour webinar of a counting system for rules that anyone can understand. Basically, if you have a play running over the right side, the center counts the third man from the outside (Diagram #9). The center

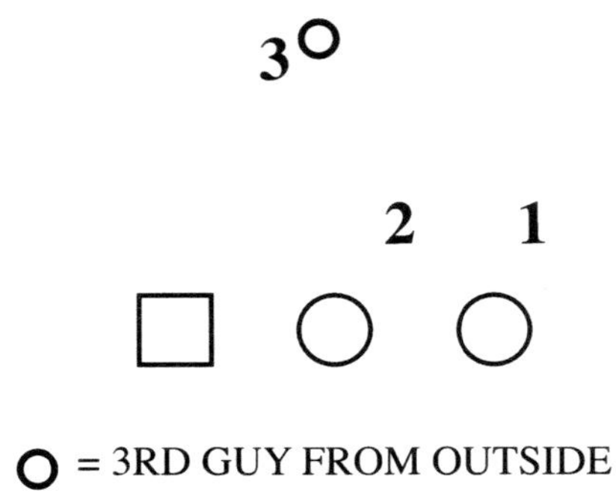

Diagram #9. C = Identify Zero

blocks the #3 defender, the guard takes the #2 defender, and the tackle has the #1 defender.

This rule is simple, as if you are appointing guys to block certain defenders. In my opinion, the only thing you can do with the different nickel fronts they give you and the multiple looks they give you is to run an unbalanced line. Otherwise, you will go crazy with everything. All of these drills are on that webinar.

CONFIDENCE IS A DECISION

A lot of the times, playing pro football has to do with confidence. What is the best way to build your confidence? The best way to build your confidence is to decide to be confident. In my opinion confidence is a decision. (Photo—Young kid on a diving board from the cover of the *Saturday Evening Post* in August of 1947.) He is going to jump, or he is not going to jump. This is a Rockwell painting that I love. This painting used to hang in my office. I think I will put it back up again.

> *A coach is the one who counts to three and makes you jump when you do not want to.*
>
> —Pavlo Sasha

That is kind of our rule as coaches.

TACKLES TURNED VS. SQUARE IN PASS PRO

Should the tackle turn, or should he stay square in pass pro? I am not talking about a jump. I am talking about a regular dropback kick slide set. You would turn if it was a jump.

BAIL POWER

First, I will show you the power Andrew Whitworth would have if he turned toward the defender. This is if he bails on the defensive end. As he turns his body toward the sideline and faces the defensive end, he does not have much power. Some players think that move is powerful when they turn toward the defender. We always want to get the players to stay as square as they can.

SQUARE AND TWIST POWER

I want to explain why blockers are stronger when they are square, facing the rusher. We call it "square and twist power." When we get out on a defender, I have more power if I am squared up on the man. If he is pushing on me, I am more powerful in my hands and arms.

When a defender is bull rushing you from the head-up position, just as important as anchoring with the feet is to take the outside hand and put it on his inside shoulder to get him off you. As his momentum comes at you, you deflect his momentum outside to take the edge off the bull rush.

Watch Whitworth as the defender comes to him. He stops the bull rush and then flattens him out to stop his momentum. When you are square, you are able to do that. You deflect the defender's momentum off you.

PASS PROTECTION DRILLS

Feet Before the Hands

We are using the technique I call "feet before hands." This is what we mean. If a defender goes inside, do not put your hands on him. Slide your feet over, and get in front of him. Then, lift with your inside hand and pick him up.

Mirror Dodge With Spacers

The players are wearing foot spacers. Where is Neil Gilman? Is Neil in here? Neil Gilman of Gilman Gear sells these foot spacers. Who invented these foot spacers, Neil? We think these foot spacers are a good thing. We worked with them this spring. Don't ask for a discount, because Neil will not give you a discount.

We line the offensive man up across from a defender. Both the offensive and defensive man has foot spacers on (Diagram #10).

Next, we have a pommel mirror drill using spacers. The defender charges the blocker, and we

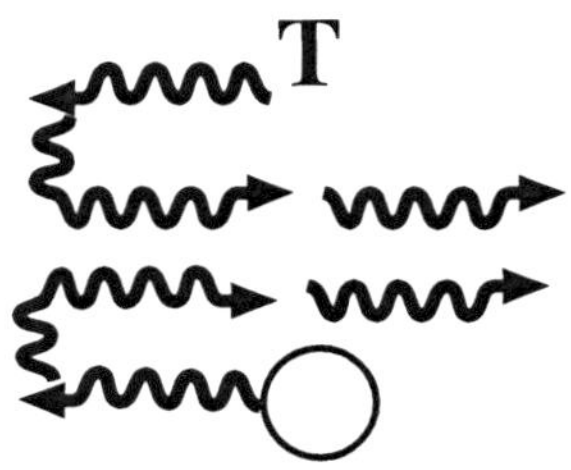

Diagram #10. Mirror Spacer Drill

block him like a top. We bring the outside arm over his shoulder, and when he makes his move, we block him like a top and turn him outside.

So we run a mirror drill with a rip, or arm-over, penetrating crossover move. The offensive man is mirroring the defensive man, and twisting him in a pommel drill. The offensive man has to lift his arm as he comes over to turn the defender. As he lifts, the inside shoulder goes down and the hand goes up. The blocker twists his shoulders as he turns the defender like a top. It is like being on a teeter-totter.

We are using the spacers in these drills. They are called "foot-spacers."

With the shuffle toss, both the defender and the blocker have the foot-spacers on. This drill is working the feet as the base, and working the hands independently. I do very little two-hand punching on any drill or block. Everything I do is done independently with the feet and hands. My feet are always set in front of the defender before I put my hands on him. You are always working to put your feet in front of the defender and then to put your hands on the man.

I'M LOST—HELP!

I am lost! (Film—Paul leading the orchestra with his baton in his right hand making the moves as the music plays.) This is kind of embarrassing.

Everything is going good right now! Everything is great. Then, right about now, I have no clue where I am with the conducting aspect of leading the orchestra. Eventually, I will find where I should be with the conducting of the orchestra. There is really no one to tell me where I am. The movement with my hands is a clue when you are lost. Right!

We need to have answers when we are lost. You know this next comment true. More times than not, the quarterback screws up the cadence. This is not a knock on any quarterbacks we have or have had; it is just a fact of football.

The quarterback may have called the play on two in the huddle. When he got to the line and started barking the cadence, it sounded as if he expected the ball to be snapped on one. The linemen have told me they knew the quarterback was mixed up, but they knew he meant for the snap count to be on one. "How in the hell did you know that?" I do not like that kind of deal. They said they could tell by the tone of the quarterback's voice. Most times, you can get away with this call. But every now and then, that technique does not work. So we came up with something that would prevent that from happening.

This is what we have. We have this built into our system. When we get to the line of scrimmage, a part of our cadence includes a color in the call. We use a color in our cadence just like a lot of other people do.

We have a special designated color in the cadence the quarterback can use that tells the other 10 players a special message. "Hey guys, I forgot the snap count. But I am calling the live snap count color; the snap will be on ONE!" Are you with me?

So if the quarterback forgets the snap count, we do not worry about it. We just have the quarterback use the color that gets everyone set to go on one. Then, we have no problem on the snap count.

I have to tell you this. I was playing with the orchestra and lost my count with the music. I went ahead and freelanced it until the end of the piece we were playing. At the end, I told them this: "These are professional musicians."

They were not aware that I had lost track of the music. The conductor had told me when I got lost to wave my hands like I knew what I was doing. The orchestra did not know I was lost. It is like a conductor's secret. If you see the conductor moving his hands in circles, you may think he is inspiring the musicians. But he could be lost.

I am just about done, but I want to cover a few more points.

IT IS A NEW WORLD

Let me leave you with this. It is a new world we live in now. The world keeps changing. Perhaps it is more violent; perhaps it is more difficult to raise kids now. Maybe!

This is my daughter's project coming up soon. My daughter is a musician. She wrote this song. It was a school project. She goes to art school. When I first heard the music, I was kind of blown away. This is what a high school kid thinks of the world right now.

I listened to the words of the song. It is about the tragedy of The Sandy Hook Elementary School shooting, which occurred on December 14, 2012, in Newtown, Connecticut. I want you to listen to the words of the song. She wrote the song right after that tragic time.

> *"On the morning of December 14, 2012, the nation woke up again to begin another day. But at 9:30 a.m. the whole world was turned upside down when 20 innocent students and six faultless adults were killed in the shocking mass murders at the Elementary School in Sandy Hook."*

> *"'I knew karate and there is always a way out,' said one child whose life was cut short by someone's ignorance. Why? How could someone be so heartless? Did he look at those children in the eye? What did he see? What didn't he see?"*

> *"Imagine getting that phone call stating your child has been murdered in the Elementary School. How could you believe? More than 26 families felt this terrible grief. By nightfall the firehouse became a gathering point for parents and family members of loved ones that would never walk this earth again."*

Imagine being the father of a 15-year-old daughter who wrote that on her perspective of the world today. The world is changing. It is difficult to know what to tell our kids. We work with our kids all of the time, and it is difficult to know all of the right answers.

I had this quote on the screen at the beginning of the lecture on my slide presentation:

> *An old man told his grandson, "My son, there is a battle between two wolves inside us all.*

> *"One is Evil. It is anger, jealousy, greed, resentment, inferiority, lies, and ego."*

> *"The other is Good. It is joy, peace, love, hope, humility, kindness, empathy, and truth."*

> *The boy thought about it and asked, "Grandfather, which wolf wins?"*

> *The old man replied quietly, "The one you feed."*

YOU ARE THE ALPHA

That is what we are. We are the leaders. In school, you are the most powerful and influential person in the entire building. We have to be the leaders to feed the good. That is the answer. That is the only answer I know. The job that we have involves more than winning football games. The job we have is leading for a great future. That is all I have, thank you!

Whoa! I lied. I have books for sale. They cost $20. It is a book titled *Perform—An NFL Coach Trains as a Concert Pianist: A Journey for Athletes, Musicians, Coaches, and Teachers*. The book contains 57 little stories. They are humorous, sad, with meanings for coaching and performing.

Thank you.

ABOUT THE AUTHOR

Paul Alexander is in his 20th straight season as Bengals offensive line coach, and he is also the team's assistant head coach, having added that designation in 2003, when Marvin Lewis took over as head coach. He has 20 seasons overall with Cincinnati, having opened his tenure with one season as tight ends coach.

Alexander's line weathered injury problems at center and left guard in 2012. Projected #1 left guard Travelle Wharton was lost for the season to a knee injury in the first pre-season game, and #1 center Kyle Cook suffered a serious ankle injury in the third pre-season contest. But Alexander had a replacement groomed for the left guard spot in second-year pro Clint Boling, who started every game. And at center, the veteran coach worked to quickly develop undrafted rookie Trevor Robinson into a promising performance before Cook was able to return for the last four games and the wild card playoff contest.

Elsewhere on the line, the situation was more stable. Left tackle Andrew Whitworth earned his first Pro Bowl berth and remained one of the team's top leaders. Right tackle Andre Smith, held back early in his career by injuries, started every game for the first time and began earning league-wide notice for the abilities that made him a first-round draft pick in 2009. And at right guard, rookie Kevin Zeitler started every game after being drafted in the first round.

The Bengals were in the NFL's top 10 in fewest sacks allowed in both 2011 and 2010, and twice with Alexander's lines, the Bengals have set new franchise records for fewest sacks allowed. Cincinnati posted a new best in the division championship season of 2005 with 21 sacks allowed, and that mark was bettered in 2007, with only 17 sacks by opposing defenses.

Also in 2012, an Alexander line supported a 1,000-yard individual rushing season for the 13th time, as running back BenJarvus Green-Ellis posted a career-best 1,094 yards in his first season with Cincinnati. Other Bengals backs to post 1,000-yard years behind an Alexander line have been Corey Dillon (six times), Rudi Johnson (three times), and Cedric Benson (three times).

On October 22, 2000, Alexander's line shared the glory of a 278-yard rushing game by running back Corey Dillon vs. Denver. It was an NFL record at the time, and it still stands fourth in league annals entering the 2013 season. Cincinnati's 407 total rushing yards in that game ranks as the fifth-highest single-game total in NFL history, and is the most rushing yards in 61 years. The last team to top it was the New York Giants, who gained 423 against Baltimore in 1950.

Alexander began his NFL coaching career in 1992 as tight ends coach of the New York Jets, under head coach Bruce Coslet. In the college ranks, he coached under Joe Paterno at Penn State and Bo Schembechler at Michigan.

Alexander's birthdate is February 12, 1960. He's a native of Rochester, New York, where he attended Cardinal Mooney High School. He played football and was an Academic All-American at Cortland State (NY), and he holds a master's degree in exercise physiology from Penn State. In 2012, he was inducted into the Cortland State Athletic Hall of Fame. Off the field, he is actively involved with the Boy Scouts and high school linemen camps.

Alexander is also a pianist, and in 2011 he authored a well-received book *(Perform)*, linking the mentality and training techniques of top athletes and musicians.

He and his wife, Kathy, have three daughters: Mary Beth, Carolyn, and Emily.

ALEXANDER AT A GLANCE

- 2003—present: Cincinnati Bengals, Assistant Head Coach/Offensive Line Coach
- 1994—2002: Cincinnati Bengals, Assistant Coach
- 1992—1993: New York Jets, Assistant Coach
- 1987—1991: Central Michigan University, Assistant Coach
- 1985—1986: University of Michigan, Graduate Assistant
- 1982—1984: Penn State, Graduate Assistant
- 1979—1981: SUNY Cortland, Offensive Tackle

ZONE ADJUSTMENTS: RUN AND PASS

University of Missouri

The first thing I am going to do today is show you our inside zone. I am going to take you through how we teach it and some of our drills. I also have some film clips, but I will run through them pretty fast because really in a spread offense, when you are standing there with four-wides all of the time, you are always dealing with what if this guy blitzes. Your edges are not protected. What I want to get to at the end is some of our answers and complements to our inside zone play.

Let me show you some of our zone stats for last year.

- Ranked 2nd in SEC rushing YPG
- Ranked 16th nationally in rushing YPG
  - ✓ 237.9 rush YPG, 5.7 avg., 35 touchdowns
- Inside Zone
  - ✓ 207 rushes, 1,191 yards, 5.75 avg.
- Outside Zone
  - ✓ 108 rushes, 624 yards, 5.78 avg.

After the season, when I went back and watched all the cutups, the outside zone had more big plays than the inside zone did. I was thinking we should be running the outside zone play a lot more than we run the inside zone.

Why do we run the inside zone?

- Double-teams
- Wide defensive ends
- Beats edge pressure
- Hits quick

When I call the inside zone, I am looking for double-teams. We used to have one zone play. When I took over as coordinator last year, we went to having an inside zone play and an outside zone play. When we had one zone play, we were always looking for edge pressure and always fanning out the blocking. When I went to the inside zone play, I was looking to get the ball downhill. I wanted to give the offensive linemen the idea that they can come off the ball and double-team the heck out of the defensive down linemen. We were looking to be aggressive.

We run it against wide defensive ends. Because we are a spread team, we have open edges a lot. We get defensive ends lined up three or four yards outside of us to try to get a good pass rush. When they get wide, we are going to use the inside zone to attack that.

When I say inside zone, for us that means our aiming point is the inside hip of the playside guard, and we are trying to get the back downhill. A lot of teams like to blitz our back. It beats him up in protection. When you hit it quick and can get the cutback in there it can help you beat the edge pressure.

The following is our teaching progression:

- Two-step contact
- Fit and roll
- Fit and drive
- Leg drive
- Finish

We work on all of these things every week and incorporate it into our drills. Some of these things we work on every day, one way or another.

The first drill is two-step contact. We work simple drills over and over again. I have tape here of half line and 1-on-1 drills. Our aiming point is the inside half of the outside number. We want to be right down the sternum with a little bit of width. If the defender plays wide at the tackle position, we are going to crank the inside hand and be strong with the inside hand and drive it out. We are going to make the back cut and read correctly.

Our basic inside zone first and second read is the defensive end to the defensive tackle. We tell our guys to blink the defensive end so if he gets pinched, we can bounce it.

In our drill, we are first looking at the lead step. We are going to keep the heel off of the ground on our first step. We want to keep flexion in our ankle and toes. His weight should be on the inside ball of his foot. We want to see him coil his hips and explode through the defensive lineman.

With the defender playing wide, we are going to lose a little bit of ground on the first step. On two-step contact, we want to work the second step up the field. We are striking on the second step up the field with our elbows in and thumbs up. We call this the "fit position." We now want to lift the defender and extend our inside hand through his inside number. To finish, we want to get leg drive and drive our feet.

Repetition with these drills is important. We are looking for contact on the second step with our thumbs up. We focus on shooting our hands and keeping our eyes back. These are not at full speed. We want the focus to be on the fit. One point to watch for is we do not want his hips to come up when he takes the first steps out of his stance. We want to see them coiled so he can gain leverage and gain position.

We carry the drill to the sled. It is a little bit tougher on a five-man sled to move it.

Now that we have worked our two steps, we now want to work our fit progression. We call this our fit and roll drill. We work for a fit position and want to focus on the lift and rolling our hips at the second step. We are pressing our hands and rolling our hips.

The next progression is the fit and drive. It is basically the same thing, and now as we drive, we are concentrating on staying in a fit position. If we get into a leaning position, he is going to get jerked around or thrown down. The blocker must engage the defender's core by lifting his arms, staying in a fit position, and driving his legs.

We can run this drill with a half line. One of my favorite things to do is have the defender try to move the offensive blocker one side or another and to knock their hands off so we have to reengage. We have to go 1-on-1 when we do that so we are not running into each other and getting people rolled up on.

The next progression is the leg drive. We work on this all of the time. We use basic drills like working the boards to see leg drive and finish. We want to overemphasize leg drive and finish. We will work on it on the sleds, looking for lift and leg drive.

Probably our favorite drill is the two-man board Drill. It works out that we have to practice on our game field a lot. We do not have room for our sled there. This is a way we have worked out that replaces our sled. We have found it to be a little more realistic. We essentially have two guys replace the sled. The first guy is there for the lift, just like you do with the sled. The second guy is directly behind the first guy with his hands on his back to simulate the weight of the sled (Diagram #1).

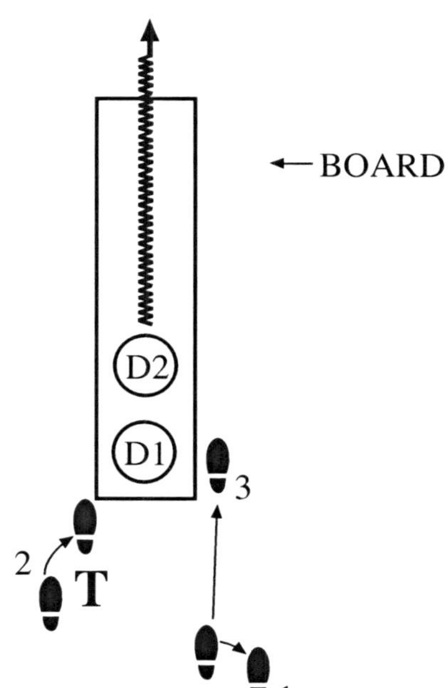

Diagram #1. Two-Man Board Drill

We are looking for the proper steps. We are looking for the lift and roll of the hips. At the snap, the blocker fits and lifts the defender off the ground. Applying resistance, the second defender keeps the first guy in the air as the blocker moves his feet. If the blocker disengages, the first guy will land on the ground because the second defender is applying the resistance. It forces the blocker to drop his hips again, drop his hands, and drive back through. This is the way we get our sled work done.

From working on our single blocks, we go to double-teams. In this drill, we are working on our combination blocks with a down lineman and a linebacker (Diagram #2). This is 2-on-2.

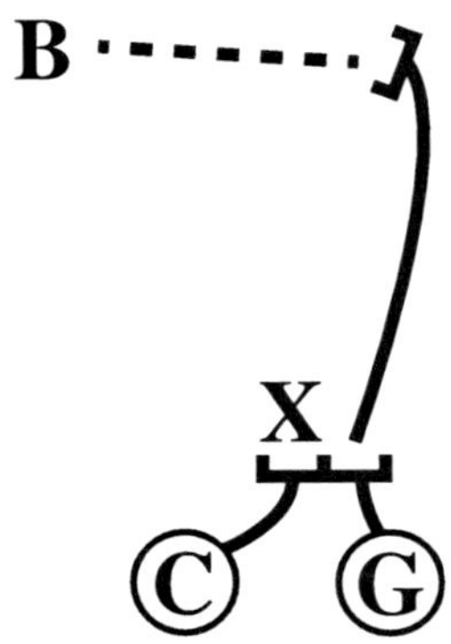

Diagram #2. Combo Block Drill

Again, we are looking at the first steps. We want contact on the second step. I want our outside guy on a double-team versus an inside shade to lower his inside shoulder as he brings his second step up the field. He is making first contact with the top of his shoulder. As we lower the shoulder, I teach those guys to take their inside hand that is making contact to tuck their hand inside and then lift with that hand. This does two things in my opinion. One, it helps you get off the block. Two, it helps to stabilize you.

We teach our inside guy on a combo block to put his eyes right on the outside tip of the defender's shoulder pads where the double-team is. Obviously, we need to get our eyes up and find the linebacker we are working to.

We drill the same way on a backside combo block. We tell the backside tackle the same thing we tell the center on the frontside double-team. We want him to take his eyes and put them on the tip of the defender's shoulder pad and drive his eyes through the block. We practice the things we are going to do in the game and we do it over and over and over again.

Next, we go into our backside cutoff blocking. We will be singled up a lot with the backside guys. The two backside guys basically use the same technique as the guard would do on a backside double-team. If the defender tries to cross our face, we will bring the second hand into it and make it a two-handed block. Again, we are looking for the second step to be up the field with contact and lift.

Inside Zone Base Rules

- Identify 4 down vs. 3 down
- Identify the Mike
- Quarterback's footwork/read
- Running back's footwork/aim point

Let me get more into the inside zone play. The quarterback is going to be at five yards. Our running back is going to be at five and a half to six. If we tell him six, he likes to scoot up and get closer to the quarterback. On the inside zone, the quarterback is going to take the ball and step to the playside at a 45-degree angle. He will turn his hips and close the back off and send him downhill into the frontside A-gap. So we do not tip off the outside zone with alignment, we align in the same position. The quarterback would then step straight back with his first step.

The running back's aim point is the inside hip of the guard. We want him to take a 45-degree angle step downhill. The lead step is with the front foot. He is blinking the outside defender, but he is riding the frontside down lineman and making his cut from there.

We are always playing off of a 4-1 box read or a 4-2 box read when we call our inside zone play (Diagram #3).

When we are in a 4-1 box read, we are going to be reading the Mike linebacker. The quarterback is reading the Mike linebacker, and we will have a quick game call. It might be bubble screen, a now screen, or whatever. Our guys know the first spot past is outside the box. We will be working the backside cutoff technique with our linemen. If the Mike comes running in, we are going to flip it out to the outside guys. If the Mike lines up tight, the quarterback can still flip it out, pre-snap.

I get asked if we do it pre-snap or post-snap. We do it both ways. Sometimes, you will see him catch the ball, turn, and just throw it. Sometimes,

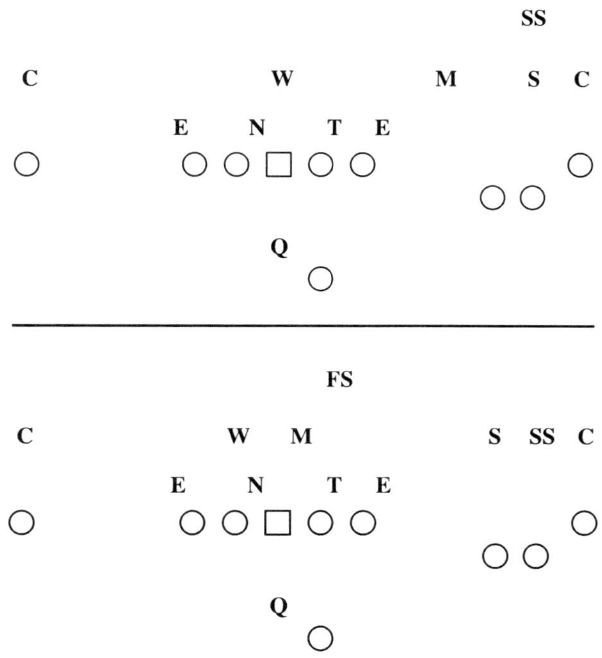

Diagram #3. 4-1 and 4-2 Box Read

you will see him catch the ball, he reads the Mike, and if he is running in, he flips his hips and throws the bubble or whatever quick game call we have made.

From a 4-2 box, if we have a full zone play called, the Will is the Mike. We are doubling on the first spot past the guards. The quarterback read becomes the defensive end. Those are the basics of what we do. We do have some plays where we are staying big on the backside no matter what. If the quarterback read is already in the box, it is telling him he is throwing it right now. Usually when we do that, we call a quick game with it. I know you are thinking, *you are calling quick game and running game, both?* Yes! It works out pretty good for us.

The quarterback knows that if the defense blitzes off the backside, he isn't protected. He is going to read the man blitzing and hand the ball off (Diagram #4). (Film)

The left tackle knows he is manned up. He is striking with the inside hand underneath with his elbows tight. We are looking for him to lift, engage the defensive ends core, and move his feet. The left guard and center are double-teaming the 3 technique and the Will linebacker. You will see the center puts two hands on the down noseguard and he gets

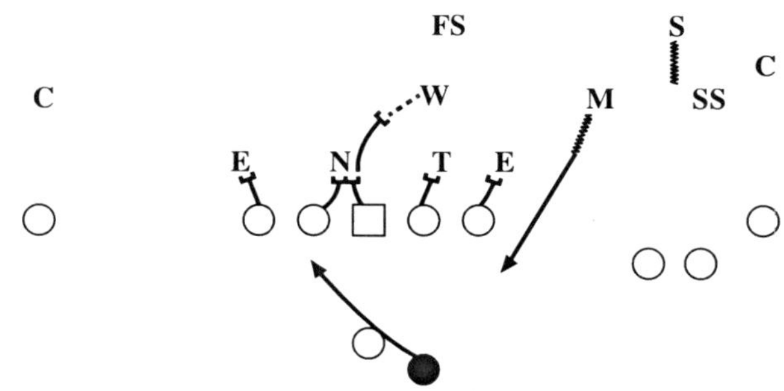

Diagram #4. 4-1 Box Blocking—Blitz

turned to the outside. I do not want to see that. He should lift with the inside hand and keep his eyes on the linebacker. He has his hips turned to the outside when the man he is to climb to is inside. He is making life hard on himself.

Next, we have a 4-2 box look (Diagram #5). The quarterback has identified the Mike and sees a 4-2 box and knows his read is the defensive end. He is looking from the top down. He sees three over three to the trips side.

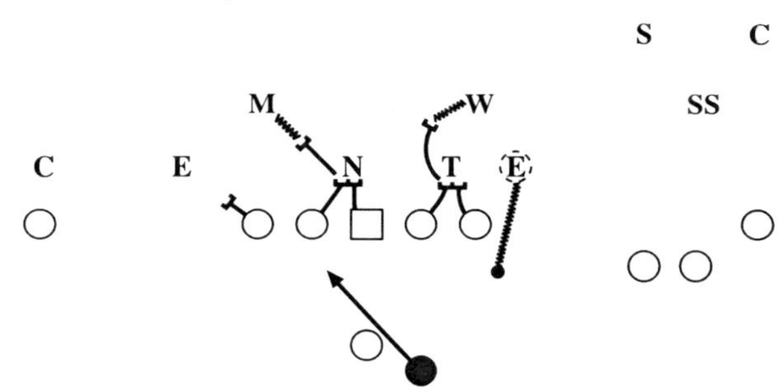

Diagram #5. 4-2 Box Blocking

The left tackle should step with his outside foot. If that guy plays wide, we are going to crank our hand and create space by driving him laterally. The left guard and center work their double-team to the linebacker. We harp on driving and getting movement. The right guard and right tackle combo the defensive tackle and Will linebacker.

Let's look at another 4-1 box (Diagram #6). In a 4-1 box, the quarterback's read is outside the box. We are going to be working through the defensive end. This is a bubble screen. Our read is moving away from the run to help with the screen so we are going to hand the ball off.

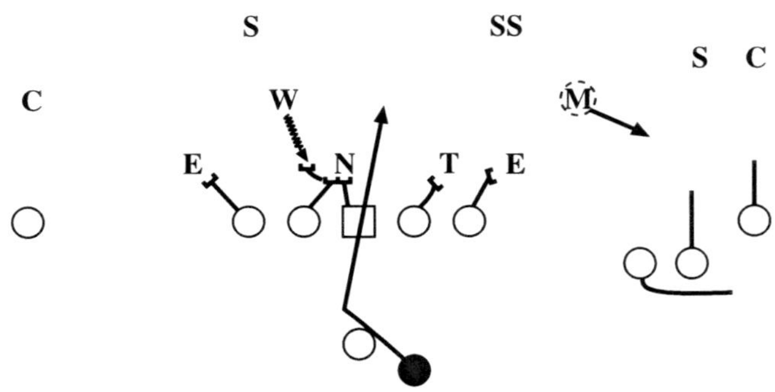

Diagram #6. 4-1 Box Read Blocking

I want to talk about tempo on the zone play.

Why We Use Tempo

- To create an advantage
- To have more plays
- To wear down our opponents
- To force the defense into quick decisions

Using an uptempo has been a huge advantage for us this year. It has especially been an advantage against teams whose personnel are really good. We practice fast all of the time, and we tell our guys by the end of the game the defense is going to be dragging. I would say about 60 percent of our practice, we are going really fast. We want to wear down our opponent.

If you are going fast, the defense will only have two or three different calls they can make. You can figure out what those are early in the game and make adjustments to just those few calls.

Our Tempos

- *NASCAR*—No-Huddle: Any formation, any play, quick tempo
- *Speed*—No-Huddle: Same formation, any play, as fast as possible
- *Lap*—No-Huddle: Same formation, same play, as fast as possible
- *Carl*—No-Huddle: Any formation, any play, QB checks play based off of certain looks
- *Pit*—Huddle: Any formation, any play, QB dictates the tempo

Our base tempo is NASCAR. We are in a hurry, but we are not sprinting. We can call any formation and any play. We are hustling to the line of scrimmage.

When we give the speed signal, that means whatever formation we were just in, line up in that formation just as fast as you can. We can look, or we can call a different play. We are sprinting to get into that formation, then they get the play, and boom off we go. We try to condense our play calls into one, two, or three words as much as possible.

If we call lap, we are going to take another lap. We are going to run the same play again. Line up and run it as fast as we can.

Carl Edwards is a NASCAR driver from Columbia, Missouri. When we go Carl, we will have some checks in by game planning. It is just like speed, but the quarterback will have one or two plays he can call based on the defense and game planning. If the quarterback can handle it, I like that. It is better than looking over to the sideline because the defense can change while he is getting the signal. When we put it into the quarterback's hands, they do not change as much.

Pit for us is just huddle up. We will huddle especially if we are ahead or trying to run some clock.

Not only are we able to run plays while the defense is turned around trying to tell each other how to line up and end up with a free six-, seven-, or eight-yard run, it is also frustrating to the defense. Our guys start laughing because the defense is yelling at each other. Our guys feed off that. Sometimes, I do not want to go fast and they come to me saying keep going faster and faster. Our kids have really bought into it and really like it.

Before I get through, let me show you some adjustments to the 4-2 box:

- Identify run support player
- Read backside run support
- Read frontside run support

You are probably saying all that stuff is great if the defense is in two high zone and you are reading the Mike. These are just some of the things we do.

Identify the run support player. He is already in the box. Having a quick game and throwing the football off of it is helpful.

Our Adjustments to a 4-2 Box

- Stretch
- Run screen
- Quick game
- Frontside read
- Play-action
- Option

To me, running the stretch out of the gun is probably the most forgiving play you can run. Plays that probably shouldn't work can turn into a 10-yard gain if you just keep working the block. You don't have to get a great block, but you have to keep working it.

I believe having the combination of both the inside zone and the outside zone gives our linemen another tool. With the inside zone, we are pounding and pounding away. The defense is firing off the ball, trying to get penetration up the field straight ahead. Our change-up is the outside zone. We are reaching them and running around them. It gives our linemen another weapon.

If we get teams that are going to overload the box by putting everybody in the box with a single high safety, then we are going to run outside zone. The quarterback is going to catch the ball and step straight back.

The aiming point for the running back is the butt of the tight end. He is reading one to two, the defensive end to defensive tackle. We tell him that by the time he gets the ball, he should already know what the first read is doing. As he is riding it, he should be reading #2. Can he hit it up in the B gap, can he get around it, or does he need to cut it back?

Let me show you the outside zone(Diagram #7). I am probably a little different in that we are blocking it a lot like inside zone. The center is going to bring his nose to the tip of the defensive tackle's shoulder pad. It is the same for the tackle and tight end. We are trying to work combinations and get around the edge. On the backside, we are doing the same thing. If we get the defender reached, we want to drive our eyes straight up the field. We do not want to turn him back because we have found they can fight off the block and get over top of you and back into the play. What could have been a 20-yard gain turns into a four-yard gain. If the defender is fighting hard

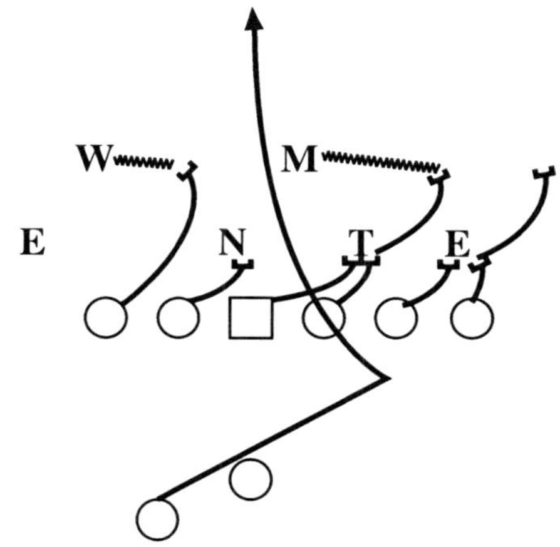

Diagram #7. Outside Zone

down the line of scrimmage, we are going three to five steps with him and then we are chopping him.

Guys, I hope you got something out of this. I thank you for your time.

ABOUT THE AUTHOR

Josh Henson joined the University of Missouri football coaching staff in February 2009, and was promoted to offensive coordinator following the 2012 season. The first new hire to join Gary Pinkel's staff since he came to Missouri in 2001, Henson came aboard to serve as co-offensive line coach.

Six of his offensive line pupils at MU have won all-star honors nine times in his tenure, including the most recent being true freshman guard Evan Boehm, who was named a First-Team Freshman All-American by *College Football News* following the recently completed season. Missouri offensive line helped pave the way to a conference team rushing title in 2011 (ranking 9th nationally), and also to a final national rank of 12th in total offense (475.54 YPG).

Henson has provided an immediate impact for the Tigers' football program, both on and off the field. The Tigers' offensive line—despite the pre-season loss of All-Big 12 left tackle Elvis Fisher to a season-ending injury—developed into a stout unit that paved the way for a Big 12 team rushing title in 2011. The Tigers ranked 9th nationally, and led the Big 12 in rushing (244.00 avg.) and also ranked 12th nationally in total offense (475.54 avg.), despite featuring a first-year starter at quarterback.

In the recruiting battles, Henson quickly helped MU establish ties to areas in which it had little success in recent years, and his efforts helped the Tigers' 2010 class to a No. 21 national ranking by Rivals.com—marking the highest ranking ever for an MU recruiting class.

Henson replaced former Tigers' coach Dave Christensen, who was the first assistant to leave Pinkel's staff since coming to MU in 2001. Christensen was named the head coach at Wyoming in December 2008.

Henson spent his four years prior to joining Missouri as tight ends coach and recruiting coordinator at Louisiana State University, where he developed the reputation as being a tremendous on-field teacher of the game, while also leading the charge for LSU's recruiting classes which ranked among the top 10 in the nation four times—including a 2009 class which ranked as No. 2 in the nation according to Rivals.com.

A former standout offensive lineman at Oklahoma State University, Henson spent 10 years as a player and coach at the university.

In 2007, Henson's coaching efforts helped LSU sophomore tight end Richard Dickson put together one of the most productive seasons at the position in school history. At Oklahoma State, Henson was instrumental in the development of Billy Bajema, who was a three-year starter for the Cowboys. As a senior in 2004, Bajema was one of the top tight ends in the country, earning first-team All-Big 12 honors. Bajema was picked in the seventh round of the 2004 NFL Draft by the San Francisco 49ers.

As a player, Henson was a four-year letter-winner with 40 career starts for Oklahoma State from 1993–97. He was a starter on the offensive line as well as team captain for Oklahoma State's 8-4 team in 1997, a squad that played in the Alamo Bowl against Purdue. He was a second-team All-Big 12 selection as a senior. In addition to being an honorable mention All-Big 12 pick as a junior. Off the field, Henson was named the recipient of the L.L. Boger Award as a senior, an honor that recognizes a student-athlete's achievement both on the field and in the classroom.

Henson graduated from Oklahoma State with a bachelor's degree in secondary education in 1998. Upon graduation, he went straight into coaching, serving as a high school football coach in Kingfisher, Oklahoma. In one season at Kingfisher, he helped guide the Yellowjackets to the state semifinals.

Henson returned to Oklahoma State as a graduate assistant in July of 1999, spending one year with the Cowboy offensive line before taking a full-time position with OSU as tight ends coach in 2001.

Henson is a native of Tuttle, Oklahoma. He and his wife Shauna have an 8-year-old son, Will, and a 4-year-old daughter, Kate. Henson lists golf, fishing, and hunting as his hobbies in his spare time.

CURRENT TRENDS IN OFFENSIVE LINE PLAY: A GAP ENTRY RUNS

Cincinnati Bengals

I want to give a lot of credit to Howard Mudd. Back in 1982, he taught me the drop-step. Now that I work for the Cincinnati Bengals, I have the ability to use their iPad. I have my own iPad that I copied a lot the plays and drills from them.

Everything I am going to show you generally comes from someone else that I thought was interesting or it was something I thought was good. I am going to move on.

I have my iPad, and I am going to go to A-gap entry runs. I have some film of the Dallas Cowboys. All I want you to look at is the backside tackle. For all of you who are teaching zone blocking, the second man in the blocking scheme should get behind the blocker on the 3 technique (Diagram #1).

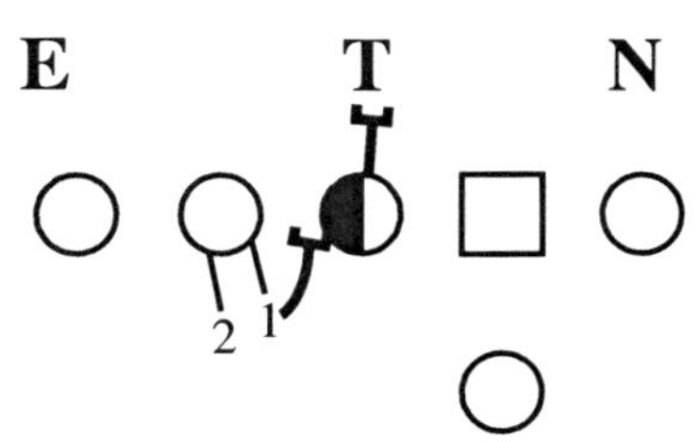

Diagram #1. Backside Tackle Zone Block

He wants to lose a step with his right foot, and lose a step with his left foot. He should step back with his inside foot, lose some ground, and then follow that with his outside foot so he ends up behind the backside guard.

If the backside tackle can lose ground and get behind the backside guard, there is no crease where the defensive lineman can penetrate the zone block. If the defender pinches, the tackle can rewind and come back and block the 3 technique.

The other thing I want to mention relates to when a man wants to use a zone block, I would encourage you not to teach the shoulder rip. When you rip the shoulder into the defender, the 3 technique flattens you out because you are mired into him. You have nothing for your buddy to fit into.

The other thing I would encourage is this: If the backside guard is working to go to the second level on the linebacker, he can afford to lose some ground. When you lose some ground and your feet are solid on the ground, and the 3 technique hits you, he will not "splash" you. These are John Strollo's words. John is the smartest guy I know. He is the line coach at Ball State University. He is my mentor, and he is younger than I am. I coached him in college.

This is the bottom line. See the right guard. If he steps up to take on the 3 technique and his feet are not on the ground, he is going to get knocked back. If he can give ground with the inside foot, take a back step with the outside foot, and come under control, when the 3 technique comes to take him on, he can stop his penetration if he has his feet set on the ground.

It is a bang, bang, bang move with his feet. He must take a quick step back and inside, move his outside foot back as he moves inside, and then get his feet up under him in a balanced stance.

And so the backside guard should get away from the 3 technique so he does not get "splashed" as the 3 technique comes inside to take on his block. If he goes bang, bang, he has a foot ahead of the other; he gets splashed.

The backside guard should get back away from the 3 technique so he does not get mired with the defender. He should use his hands against the defender. When the 3 technique attacks him, he can use his hands to throw him to the frontside, and the ball will cut behind the backside guard.

It may sound confusing, as most coaches are teaching the backside guard to use the shoulder pry with the flipper lift. When this happens, the 3 technique flattens out the backside guard and into the A-gap and stops the play. So we are talking about the over gap technique by the next blocker over. It is something to think about.

I want to talk about angle A pass blocking. Again, we are looking at the left tackle. This is the technique discussed by Howard Mudd. The tackle is blocking the wide defender on the line of scrimmage. It is against a flat set. I call that angle A (Diagram #2.) My point is: we want to take the defender on short. The defender is outside wide. This technique can be used by a guard that has to fan out against a 3-4 alignment.

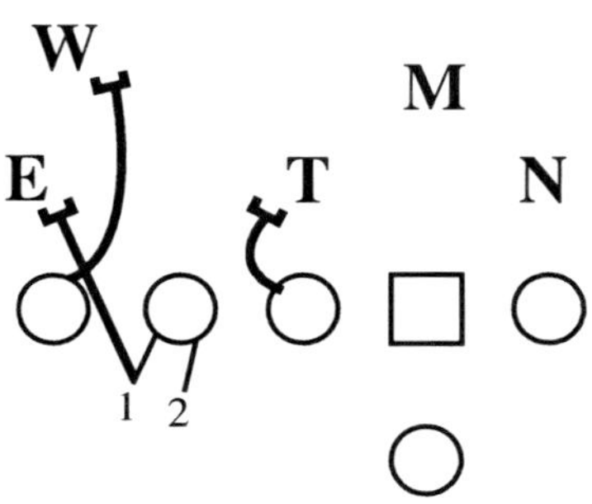

Diagram #2. Angle A Pass Protection

The key is: the tackle wants to take the defender on short. Because the defender is outside wide, and the tackle is going so flat to jump the defender in Howard Mudd's words. Because the tackle is so flat, where do you think he is vulnerable? Is it inside or outside? It is inside. If the tackle is so flat on the block, he does not have separation to recover. When we have a flat set, there is big lane between the blocker and defender.

We teach the tackle not to go so far outside against the defender. He should only take one-quarter of the defender on the block. This will cut down on the space of the lane between the tackle and the defensive man on the outside.

When the tackle is outside with the defender, he does not have to get his inside eye to the inside eye of the defender. All of the crap about getting eye-to-eye and crotch-to-crotch is bullcrap. He is protecting the inside. We want to be able to get our extended arm on the defender before he takes two steps. Trust me!

If I were not worried about having a tight end, I would use this block every time. However, if you have a big slow tackle who has slow feet, then nothing is going to work. If you have a halfway decent athlete you can take a flatter angle. The 45-degree angle is A, and a little deeper angle is B; and on and on.

Do we have any questions of the angle of the short tackle short setting against an outside rusher? Notice the left tackle did not drop-step and run outside. He took a step sideways. He is going laterally and he uses his outside arm to get to the defender. It does not matter what the defender does, the blocker has rerouted the defender.

Question: Does the tackle delay on his step outside?

The tackle wants to get his hands on the defender as soon as he can. It is a lateral step with the outside foot, a shuffle step with the inside foot, and boom! He makes contact with the defender. The blocker wants to get his hands on the defender before the defender can get his hands on the blocker. The blocker does not wait on the defender to move.

Next, I want to talk about the Bengals' double-team block. On the film we are looking at, the defensive 3 technique on the tight end side of the formation. It is J.J. Watt of the Houston Texans. He was being double-teamed by the Bengals, but he was splitting the double-team block.

Again, this is the concept from John Strollo of Ball State. He is my mentor, and he is 10 years younger than I am. I coached him at Boston College. This is how the Bengals double-team blocked J.J. Watt.

The offensive guard is going to deliver force without momentum (Diagram #3). Watch his feet. His feet move, but they do not go anywhere. He just moves his feet in place. His hands are in front of him. You are stronger when your feet are behind you or underneath you, with a good base. That is when I am strongest. You are never stronger when one foot is in front of you.

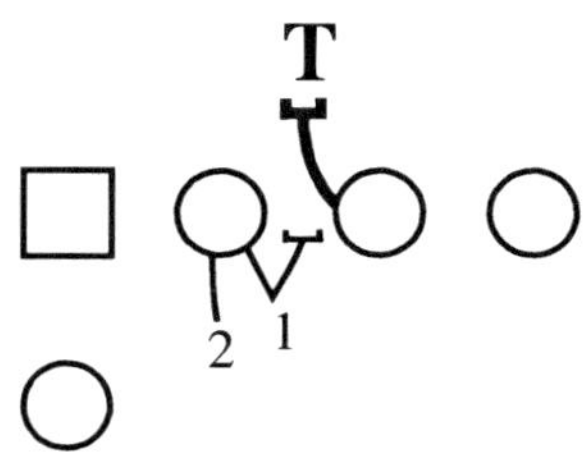

Diagram #3. Force Without Momentum

His feet are under him or behind him, his hands are in front of him, and he has a big chest. Obviously, he has a 350-pound tackle that is on the double-team block with him. Watch what the right guard does. He is using force without momentum. His upper body goes forward, but he runs in place with his feet. His hands are forward, and the double-team block works.

I want to move on and look at some film on the Washington Redskins. I call this section "Redskins Critical Points." Let's look at the left guard. The guard has no help on the play (Diagram #4). Watch where the left guard's right hand is placed? The guard did not set to the inside, but that is where he is vulnerable. You cannot get beat inside, and this is an example of that happening.

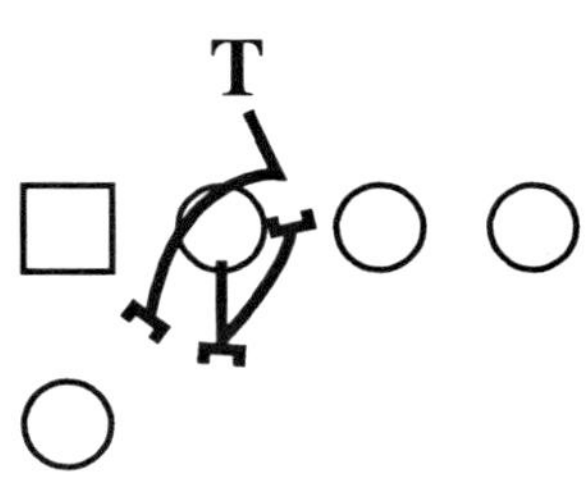

Diagram #4. Getting Beat Inside

I want to show you another example of the right guard blocking on a 3 technique (Diagram #5). This is how Howard Mudd taught the block. You can use this

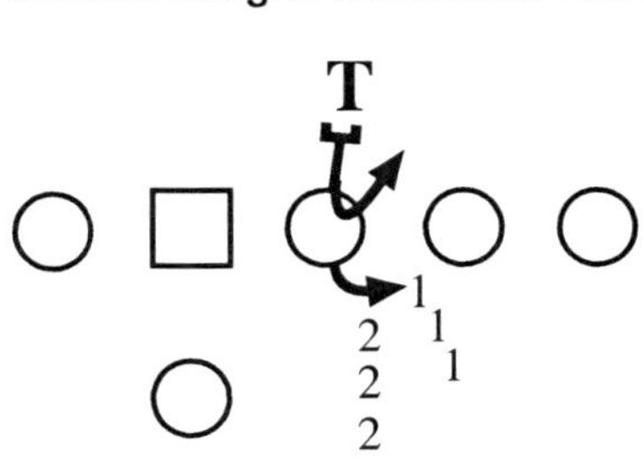

Diagram #5. Blocking the 3 Technique

technique every time. The guard jumps the defensive 3 technique. What do we notice about his feet? How fast are they going? They are going 100 mph.

All he is doing is closing the space between him and the defender. He still has the posture, his back arched, his feet firing. All he did was to move his body to a position where he could block the 3 technique. He only goes part-way out on the man. If the defender goes inside or outside, he can still recover and block the man. He keeps his center of gravity.

Most players that use the jump to get to the 3 technique go too far on the jump and go into the defender. Like Howard Mudd would say, "Close the space." Watch the left hand. He puts it on the shoulder point and puts his hands in the middle of the chest.

Let's look at the left tackle. We discussed the A angle block. The left tackle went too far on his steps outside (Diagram #6). When that happens, it allows the defender to cut back inside. Don't go so far outside on that situation. When the tackle goes flat farther outside, he should use his outside hand. That is an example of the blocker going too far outside on the 5 technique.

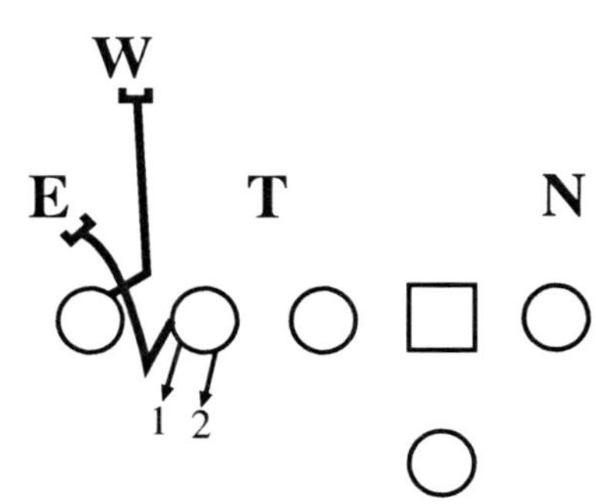

Diagram #6. Blocker Steps Too Wide

As long as the blocker is slightly inside of the defender and uses his outside hand, he can make the block. The outside hand is the closest hand to the defender. If you do this, you can disrupt the defender's momentum.

You do not want the quarterback to get killed on a pass play. The offensive man must know how far to go outside on the angle block. He must get the inside hand ready to use against the inside rush.

This is Howard Mudd's stuff. We see the right guard getting bull rushed. He has his left hand inside on the shoulder point. He would have been better off if had jumped like he did before. For whatever reason, he did not jump the 3 technique. He does a good job of anchoring down on the block.

We have another shot of the right guard blocking the 3 technique. He does a good job of taking two steps up, gives a head fake, and takes an inside swat at the 3 technique. Whatever move the 3-technique has, the right guard has an answer. He has a strong inside arm. He is taking it to the defender. It may be under the armpit, or on the shoulder point. What I am saying to the guard is to get the inside arm ready. It does not matter if he clamps it, or clubs it like Paul Alexander teaches, it does not matter.

I want to go to drills by John Strollo. He knows more football than anyone I know. He was the tight end coach at Penn State last year. Now, he is the offensive line coach at Ball State. Go see him, or study the Ball State films, or whatever. He will blow your mind. You will be saying, "Why couldn't I have thought of that?"

The first drill is with the right guard blocking on a 3-technique defender. The 3 technique is not coming at the guard. The defender has a medicine ball chest high for the blocker to aim for. He has two feet behind him after the first two steps. He is not going forward and then going after the defender. When he makes contact with the defender, his feet are underneath him (Diagram #7). His feet are really behind him. That is where we are the strongest.

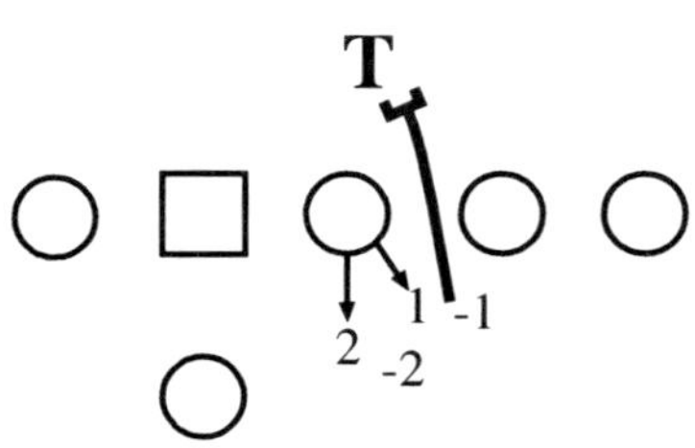

Diagram #7. Guard—Feet Underneath His Body

You are the strongest when you are using your anchors. Your anchors are either the hands in front of you or your feet behind you. It is not one foot ahead of the other. It could be your head if you have short arms. If you have your feet underneath your body, and have your arms in front of you, when the 3 technique rushes, you will not get splashed.

Coach Strollo is practicing the different drills in the film. We have a center, and he has a defender that is in a shade technique. We all must understand about using the short chopping small steps in a balanced position.

The hands of the blockers are so close to their body. The blockers wear "small meatballs" on tennis balls on their hands.

If the defender can get the blocker with one foot forward, he is going to knock the blocker on his butt. If your feet are not under you when you strike, you are going to get knocked back. This is a fact, and it is not something I invented.

In the old days when we blocked against a defender outside, we all lost ground. But we only lost ground with one foot, right?

Let me talk for a few seconds about the mid-zone blocking. The play may be a stretch play going to the open side. It is not a wide play, and it is not an up-the-gut play. It is a stretch play going in the C gap, or to the outside leg of the tackle (Diagram #8). The blocker steps back with the outside leg. Then, he loses ground as he moves both of his feet. Then, it is boom, boom, and now he has his inside arm under the armpit of the defender. He is not going to let the defender redirect.

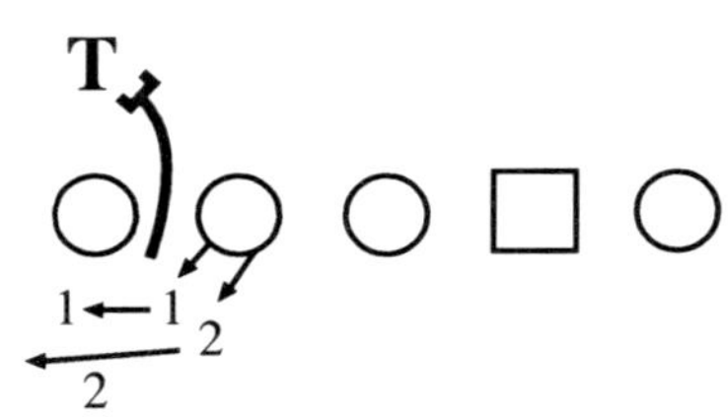

Diagram #8. Mid-Zone Block

It does not make a lot of difference if he places his inside arm under the armpit or if he plants it on the tip of the shoulder. It does not matter. He wants to define the defender and to keep him to the outside. He does not want him to come inside, where he would have to retrace the defender.

Next, we look at the center blocking a man on his nose in more of a stretch play (Diagram #9). We watch the center's feet. He is coming back two steps. When he makes contact with the nose man, his feet are behind him. The bottom line is this. He is using a backside one arm long-arm block.

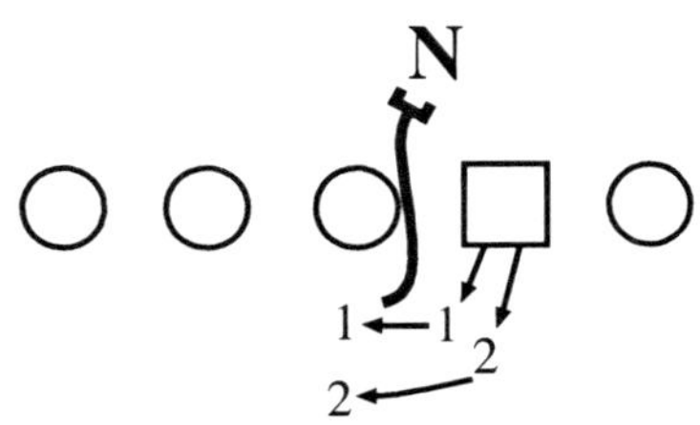

Diagram #9. Center Stretch Block

We used to think we had to blow off the ball and take a lead step toward the defender and reach the man on the second step. Now, we want to lose ground with the first two steps and give ground as we move closer to the defender. We want to lock the arm out. When the nose man hits the blocker, he has his feet under him and he can absorb the contact and not get knocked off balance.

I do not know all of the terms used by physiologists because I do not know all of the physical concepts, but I do know when your legs are behind you, it is when you are the strongest.

Someone coaching like we did in the 1950s may say I am crazy, but you have to keep up with the times. All I know is this: In watching one of the best centers in football, his feet are behind him when he executes the mid-zone block.

Next, I want to look at bend plays. We are going to review some predetermined cutback plays (Diagram #10). We are giving the defense the illusion

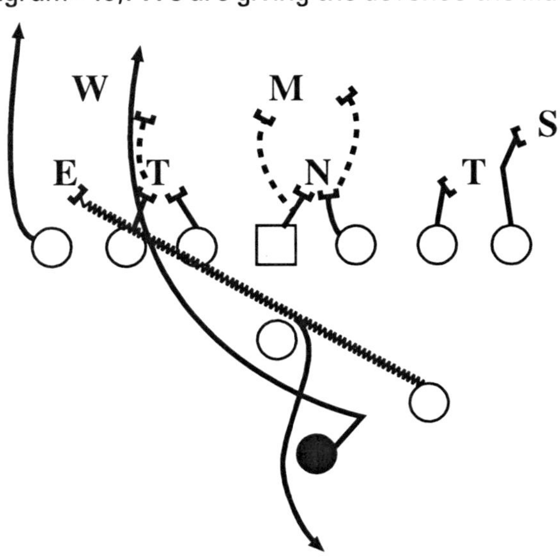

Diagram #10. Bend—Cutback Blocking

that we are running the inside zone play. The offset back is coming across the formation to block the end outside. The split end is running a pattern to make sure someone is defending the flat. The guard and tackle are blocking the play as if it were the inside zone play. The backside guard wants to use his hands to force the 3 technique inside.

If you run the zone read plays, you can run the play to the weakside or the strongside. You can tell the offense, "we are going to run the zone play, but we are going to make it a cutback play." You can call it "bend" or "cutback." It does not matter, but it looks like the zone read play.

The ball is going to cut behind the block of the guard and tackle, and inside the defensive end. That is the cutback play. I just wanted to mention it to give you something to think about.

From the bend, we are going to look at our 93 McNally scissors/Sam play. The term scissors in this usage means we are handing the ball off over the top, and behind the quarterback. On the bend, we are handing the ball off in front of the quarterback.

If we call "93 scissors Sam," we are telling the fullback to block the Sam linebacker (Diagram #11). We have the onside guard and tackle block the Mike linebacker. So the blocking assignment we are using is as if we were running a one-back play to the open side of the formation. The onside line must take care of the Will Linebacker. It is a pre-determined cutback play. If you have a good running back, the misdirection play is good for the offense.

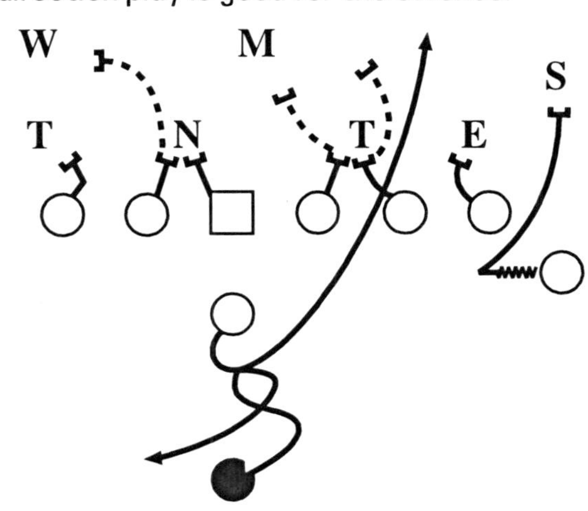

Diagram #11. 93 Scissors Sam

Next is the P scissors (Diagram #12). Now we are going to pull one of the offensive linemen. We are going to look at the G play going to the tight end side. The guard on that side pulls on the play. We are giving the misdirection opposite of the pulling guard.

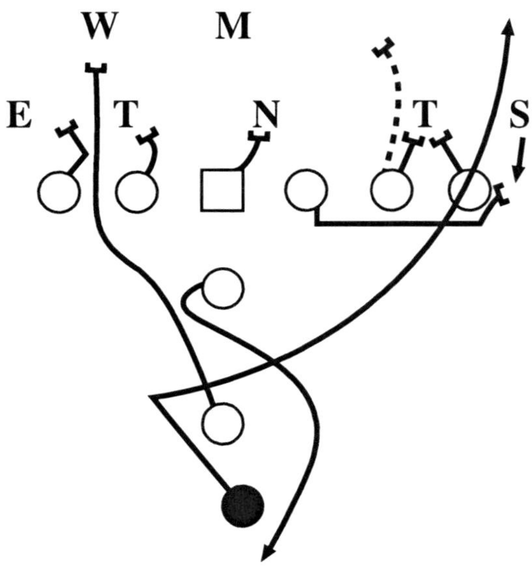

Diagram #12. Guard P Scissors

The defense does not play the guard P scissors play as well when they see full flow to the opposite side of the pulling guard. This play is similar to a two-back zone play with a lead block by a back.

Question: Do you ever pull the center on this play?

We could pull the center, depending on the defense. These plays end up as big plays, and I do not understand why more teams do not run them.

I did a study on the Philadelphia Eagles this past year. I am going to be talking about little steps again. I am encouraging you to write this name down. John Strollo, offensive line coach of Ball State. This is what he teaches.

Best Block

- Hands in front together
- Big chest
- Feet underneath
- Little steps

Moving to techniques taught by Howard Mudd, we have a film clip on a former center from the University of Cincinnati. His name is Jason Kelce. He has two feet under him when he makes contact with the nose guard. Where are his hands? They are in front of him. What about his chest? He has a big chest, right? He uses little steps and has his feet behind him. That is the technique we like.

I have another film clip of a guard taking big steps in blocking against a 3 technique (Diagram #13). He takes big steps and his back is bulled forward just a little. He gets beat because he has one foot in front, and he defender over powers him. (Film)

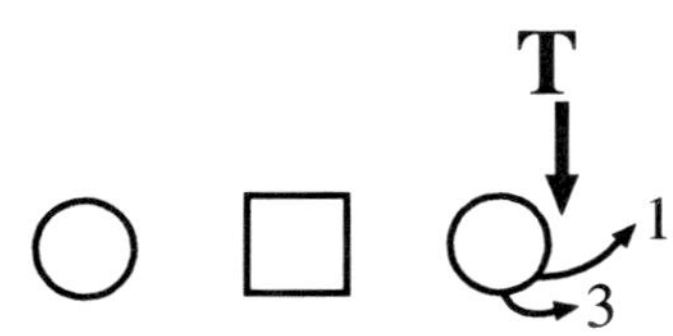

Diagram #13. Big Steps on Block

Are we good with little steps, feet behind the butt, and all of the other points we have covered?

Next, we have an example of a blocker that has separation on the defender. It is on a stretch play. He is trying to hook the 3 technique. The point I want to make is this. If you can get separation with your inside hand, you can turn the defender outside. Or you can work the hips to get square on the defender. The time and space gives the blocker that option.

We have separation, and we can stay in place if the defender is running outside like a bat out of hell. But if the blocker mires into the defender and tries to hook him, he may not be successful. The guard is using a reach block using separation to start with.

There is something about using the long-arm technique. We have a saying that goes like this: "One arm is longer than two arms." I feel certain you know about that quote.

In the five minutes that I have left, I want to talk about a general run study we did. We have a receiver in a 1-on-1 drill. When he blocks the defender, where are his feet? They are behind him. This is not going to happen a lot, right? Where are his hands? They are in front of him. What kind of chest does he have? He has a big chest. He wins with that block.

We are looking at the center against a nose man. As he makes contact, he has his feet under him, and he is climbing the defender. I am talking about the finish on the block. I do not care if you call it double under, climbing, or lifting. He has a grab on the defender. He is blocking against a big-ass noseguard. Hopefully, you can see the demeanor on the block.

I want to move to some blocks the Bengals are using. I want to brag on Paul Alexander for a minute. I am going to talk about the Bengals' pass pro ideas. We are watching the right guard. On the jump-set, he has his inside arm up where he can apply pressure on the defender.

As another example, watch the left guard. Watch his left hand. His outside hand, or his left hand, is in position to move to the inside shoulder of the defender.

When the defender goes inside, and this is for all of you that have done the post foot thing, what do you do with your inside foot when the defender goes inside? The best thing is to pound the post foot and to drop it because that is the only way you can stay in front of the defender.

You can see that Coach Alexander wants the blocker to get his inside hand to that club position that he talked about.

As soon as the blocker hits the defender, and gets his hand on the inside of the defender, he may want to separate because the defender may not be rushing.

When the defender goes inside, if you do not get the punch on the man, he should take the inside hand and clamp him, and work the hips inside. As Paul Alexander would say, "Block him like a top."

I did not cover as much material as I had planned. We know that Paul does a great job with the offensive line for the Bengals.

At this time, I am going to bring up Scott Peters so he can give you some of the things that are happening in other phases of athletics related to football.

I coached Scott Peters with the New York Giants. When he came out of Arizona State, at the combine he benched 42 times the amount of weight they used for that test. He will tell you today that he does not even believe in the bench press. He is the world champion in jujitsu in his weight class. He is one strong dude.

I took a liking to this guy because he is a tough SOB. He is one of the few guys that played in the NFL that, and I will tell you there are some, but he actually knows how to coach. Most players will tell you they did things this way and that way. He has what he calls quick, twitch, movements. Watch him. He usually tries to do the same thing that Paul Alexander does. Watch him as he talks about the way he moves his hips and hands.

ABOUT THE AUTHOR

Throughout Coach Jim McNally's career, he was one of the most highly regarded position coaches in the league. McNally made an immediate impact on every team when hired to coach their offensive line.

With the Bills in 2005, McNally helped second-year tackle Jason Peters develop into a starter. Peters, an undrafted free agent and former tight end at the University of Arkansas, started the final nine games of the season at right tackle. The line paved the way for Willis McGahee's career-high 1,247 yards.

With the Bills in 2004, McNally tutored an offensive line that limited opponents to 38 sacks, the lowest number allowed by a Bills team since 1998. Also with the Bills, McNally's line also paved the way for Willis McGahee to rush for 1,128 yards and 13 touchdowns in 11 starts.

Prior to retiring from the NFL with the Bills, McNally coached the offensive line for the New York Giants (1999–2003) and helped maintain offensive line success with little personnel continuity on the line during his tenure. In 2000, McNally guided an offensive line with three new players to a successful season, which culminated in the Giants' rise to the NFC championship.

Prior to joining the Giants, McNally coached the offensive line for the Carolina Panthers (1995–1998) and the Cincinnati Bengals (1980–1994). In McNally's time at Carolina, the Panthers advanced to the NFC championship game in only the team's second season of existence.

McNally's longest tenure was as the offensive line coach for the Cincinnati Bengals. In his time at Cincinnati, McNally helped establish one of the most potent rushing attacks in the league from 1986 to 1990. He coached Hall of Fame offensive tackle Anthony Muñoz, and the Bengals advanced to the Super Bowl two times during his tenure.

Before entering the NFL coaching ranks, McNally coached the offensive line at Wake Forest (1978–1979), Boston College (1975–1977), and Marshall University (1971–1974). McNally initiated his coaching career at his alma mater, University at Buffalo, and coached there for six seasons (1965–1970).

NFL teams have hired McNally to be a consultant to the football staff. He spent the 2010 and 2011 football seasons with the New York Jets. He started work with the Cincinnati Bengals in 2012 and 2013.

Originally from Buffalo, McNally played guard at the University at Buffalo from 1961 to 1964, and the combination of his playing career and his coaching expertise earned him a spot in the university's Hall of Fame. Now retired from coaching, Jim is nationally known for his clinics on offensive line coaching, which he conducts in the off-season.

MUDD'S METHODS: OFFENSIVE LINE TECHNIQUES PROVEN TO WORK

NFL Alumni

Thank you for inviting me here to speak today. I didn't start out coaching because I had a passion to do it. I stumbled into it. Once I started doing it, I loved it. I have since retired, and now I love riding my motorcycle more than anything else. My wife said to me one day, "Howard, when you get on the phone and you start talking about football, your eyes light up. Something happens to you." I do like talking about football, and I am very passionate about it.

If you can come to this clinic and get anything from every one of us, I do not care if it is one word, you have profited. What you may get is a validation of what you have done or are already doing. You may think you didn't gain any new knowledge, but trust me, just having what you are doing validated is important. I hope you understand that.

Quickly, a little bit about my background. I was a player and all that stuff. I want to show you a few people who played a part in my evolution. The first guy is Tiger Johnson. Tiger coached for the Bengals. He was the guy that gave me belief in myself when I was a player. He was a tough and cerebral guy and helped me look at football in a cerebral way. If someone came up to me and said you remind me of Tiger Johnson as a coach, I couldn't be more proud. Two other guys on my list are Merlin Olsen and Alex Karras, who I played against in the league, and I had some success against them. The other is Ernie Zwahlen. He almost ran me out of ever thinking about being a coach. He said everything was wrong that you did in the past, and you were only going to do it his way. He only lasted four or five years in the league. He ticked me off so I had to put him on there.

Last year, I helped coach a high school team since I had retired from the NFL. I helped at Mount Si High School in North Bend, Washington. Those boys at Mount Si High School got it and they understood it.

Definition of an Offensive Lineman

- The only members of any sport that do not see the object of the game (ball)
- Learned skills
- Who do I get? How do I get him?

We teach skills. Talent is something you are born with. As coaches, we teach skills so skills are something that you learn. Our guys have to learn angles, body position, applied techniques, and fundamentals.

My whole thing is to take a few things and do them extraordinarily well. If they put that on my gravestone, I would love that.

- Focus on the task, not the result—repetition.
- Slow the game down (Bird/Lilja).
- Easier to fix the problem with one method.

Larry Bird was a pretty good foul shooter. He wanted you to follow him toward the end of the game because he was going to make you foul him. He was going to make the foul shots and put it on you. *Sports Illustrated* ran an article on Larry Bird when he was younger, and he shot a thousand free throws every day. Does anybody remember that? That is a lot of free throws. He talked about the basket being so big at a critical moment in time. Do people raise their level of performance at a critical time? I do not believe that people do. I believe the great ones do what they do regardless of the stress and they let everybody else mess their pants. You don't raise your level, you just keep practicing and you slow the game down.

The other guy's name is Ryan Lilja. Lilja was a guard for us when we won the Super Bowl. He was a little bitty guy with short arms. Ryan was one of my favorite players ever. He could block the crap out of you. In Indianapolis, we practiced against a fast, uptempo offense. They were all over the place. We were going to play the Tampa Bay Buccaneers with their famous defensive coordinator. Their defense ran all of these games, and Coach John Teerlinck didn't think we could block them. We started playing them, and Ryan Lilja came off the field after the first series and said something was wrong. I said, "What do you mean?" He said we were beating them to the punch. I started laughing at him. We practiced at the speed we practiced at, so it made the game easier and slowed the game down for them.

That is what you should be after. Slow the game down, and focus on the task. Forget about the result. Put your foot down in the right place and focus on the right thing. Where are you going to put your hands? Where are you going to put your foot? Focus on that, and the game slows down.

If you just focus on a few things and try to do them well, it becomes easier to fix the problem. I know this is contrary to some other things you have heard in these clinics. Hang on to your hat.

Stuff That Works

- Three-, five-, and seven-step is a myth—same dish.
- Jump to level the playing field vs. better athletes. You get to them before they get to you.
- Set short or shorter. Every pass is a play-action pass, aggressive.

Let me get started with some pass protection concepts. There is only one way to pass protect for me. One way! I am talking about concepts of technique. It does not matter if it is a three-step, five-step, or a seven-step drop. If you look at the logic and the angles of it, it is all the same. We are going to set real short and aggressively.

Every play is a play-action pass for me. You are going to set short, or you are going to set shorter. In a play-action pass, the harder you hit him, the more he sticks to you. That is as simple as pass protection can be for a play-action pass. You are going to go after the guy all of the time.

If you have multiple sets and you face multiple problems, you have to figure out a solution to each of those problems from each of those different sets. I want to be real simple. Our job is to make complicated and complex systems, concepts, and techniques into something simple so they understand them and can repeat them and have success.

More Stuff That Works

- Stance: Saigon squat, flat-footed, toe out.
- Natural sequence of motion. No robots.
- Little bitty baby steps to overcome inertia.
- Toe out (it's natural)
- Play with your feet; the rest of the body gets in the way.

In Vietnam, they used to squat and crap in a hole. I used to test people by making them spread their feet in a stance and squat and touch their thumb on the ground. You get flat-footed with the toes out. If you observe somebody standing out in the hall shooting the bull, you can picture their feet are out at an angle. We don't stand with our feet parallel. We eventually create robots when we put kids in an unnatural stance.

I am looking for a flat-footed stance. I want to see toes out and cleats in the ground. I want the feet on the ground as soon as they can be after each step. You want to be able to overcome inertia when you are stuck. If you take little bitty baby steps you can accomplish that.

Additional Stuff That Works

- Run Blocking—press him away from you.
- Pass Protection—press yourself away from him.
- Problem Solving—think outside the box.
  - ✓ Hop, spin, drag arm

According to Vince Lombardi, the difference between a good block and a great block is the interval between contact and drive. Most blocks are stalemates. The initial contact is a stalemate, at least in high school they are. What are you going to do next? In run blocking, when you are stuck on a man, take little bitty baby steps and start moving your feet. When he moves and starts to go, press him away from you.

In pass protection, you are going to go get him and then, when you are stuck, press your chest away from him so you can redirect yourself laterally.

I am a hop guy. Immediately when you feel pressure, you should start to hop. If I have my hands on the defender and I feel pressure in my hands, I am going to hop, hop, and get my butt down. It is just a quick short hop backward. I want to get leverage and get my center of gravity a little lower than his. This makes him fight through all of my shock absorbers—hands, arms, shoulders, and all that stuff. If you have a nice coil, you can do that.

One day, I was trying to figure out how I wanted to teach pass protection. I was tuned into a NBA game with the Celtics. I watched Dennis Johnson who was a great defensive guard for the Boston Celtics. Offensive players would start backing down defenders from the top of the key. Dennis would put a hand on the players back and would take a short hop back as he would feel pressure. You were allowed to hand check back then. He would hop back with his toes out, and he was able to move. That is the origin of my philosophy on the hop. Most of the stuff I know about comes from trying to solve a problem.

If you are a left tackle and you have to watch a 3 technique for a stunt but have to block the defensive end, you are caught in the middle. If you drag your arm, you can go get the defensive end, and if the 3 technique comes, you will feel him with your drag arm before you have to block him.

If you have a tight end stunt, and you try to throw him but don't throw him enough, what are you going to do? You are stuck there and can't get off him. You can wait until you get to the sideline to get you butt chewed because you didn't throw him hard enough. If you just spin with your back to him, you will come right back in front of him. Defensive backs do it all the time. Why can't offensive linemen do it?

Mental Stuff That Works

- Valley of Darkness—focus on task and not results. Find each player's triggers.
- Don't be afraid to succeed. Can't be overly critical of a young guy if he makes an effort to get it right.
- Okay is part of success. Young players need to know they're on their way.
- Take risks, encourage them to take chances.

We teach players specific techniques, and they finally get it. Then all of a sudden, they start thinking, and they aren't worth a darn because they start thinking. They start thinking about the result and not the task. You can tell those guys because they have a blank look. You have probably had that same blank look at one time yourself, or have coached players with that blank look. They become terrified of failing. They have been successful in the past. The only way out of that situation is to come back to the task. I use little triggers to help me. I used to say to myself, "Feet and numbers." I wanted to remember to move my feet and to see the numbers. Big guys might remind themselves to keep their belt down. I told Ryan Lilja, "Quit looking at the guy's chest; talk to yourself." Use little triggers for that which is causing one to remain in the valley of darkness.

Get your guys to take a chance and encourage them to do so. Let them know that they can improve by taking a chance. Let them know that "okay" is part of success. Stop coaching them on every play for what they are to do.

Let me go over the vertical set versus the dish (Diagram #1). The dish is an elliptical thing. The trapezoid is the vertical looking thing. The quarterback is in the same spot for both.

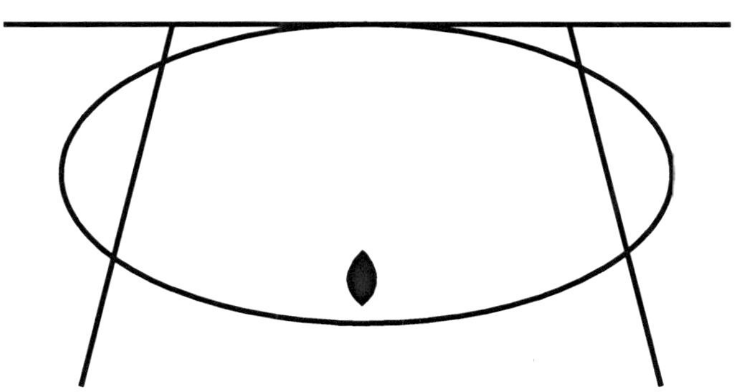

Diagram #1. Vertical vs. the Dish

You want to get your hips on the dish to start off with. You want to distort or flatten the guy out to the end of the ellipse. If you set in the vertical and the rush is from the outside, you have to turn your shoulders along the trapezoid. That is essentially two movements. I say: why don't you just go to the spot where you will intercept the defender and shorten the distance. I am not going to get square first.

As I said earlier, three-, five-,and seven-step, it is a myth (Diagram #2).

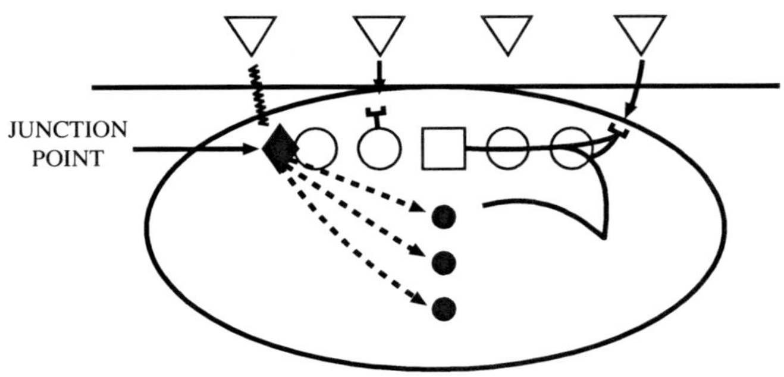

Diagram #2. Three-, Five-, and Seven-Step = Same Technique

If you look at the 5 technique and our left tackle, the junction point where I am going to go out and take that guy on is virtually the same, regardless of how deep the quarterback is. If you are an offensive lineman, how do you really know where the quarterback is? The guy you are blocking tells you exactly where the quarterback is. Jump his butt, flatten him out, and keep him in front of you. We are going to set in the same place regardless of where they tell me the quarterback is going to drop to.

If you look at the defender outside the right tackle, I am illustrating that you want to keep resetting that guy parallel to the dish. Flatten him out along the lines parallel to the dish.

Reasons for the Dish

- Provide the quarterback with separation from the rush.
- Keep the pocket from collapsing on the quarterback.

Pass Protection Principles

- Rhythm = Aggressive, passive, aggressive (fast, slow, fast)
- Dish, not pocket
- Shake hands (engage)
- Redirect (hop-hop), (lag)
- Finish (flatten him out)
- Distort line of deployment

The rhythm of pass protection is aggressive, then it is passive, and then it becomes aggressive again. For a tackle setting, it would be fast, slow down and settle, and then fast again. It all happens pretty quickly, but get out there to reduce the distance. Get to them before they get to you. They are better athletes than you are, go jump them. Level the playing field.

The position you want is a handshake position from wherever that defender starts out. I do not care how you do it; you want to go shake hands with him. Once the defender is ready to head toward the quarterback, I want my hips and my shoulders parallel to his. I do not want to backpedal, decide where he is coming from, and then get parallel to him. That is too many moves and takes too much time. I want to get out there in front of him, and if we were to shake hands with our near arm, that is the position I want to be in. We have a drill where we take our first step and just patty cake with the defender. That gets us in the correct position. If you do that a hundred times a day, you might get better at getting into the position you want to be in.

You want to reduce distance and get to him. Once I get on you, if you want to go to the inside, that is okay because I am just going to flatten you down along the dish. Distort his line of deployment. That is just a fancy way of saying I am going to flatten you out along the dish regardless of which direction you want to go.

I want to talk about the cylinder (Diagram #3). I want to think of every player as a cylinder. If the quarterback was to take a cleaver and, from his angle, split the defender down the middle, it would not be between the numbers. It would be slightly offset to the inside of the cylinder. The farther outside the defender is, the more the offset is to the cylinder. I want you as a blocker to take your Pinocchio nose and put it right on the middle of the cylinder with both hands equal distance on both sides of that. Hey, that coincides with shaking hands with me. It is the same thing. Find the middle of the cylinder.

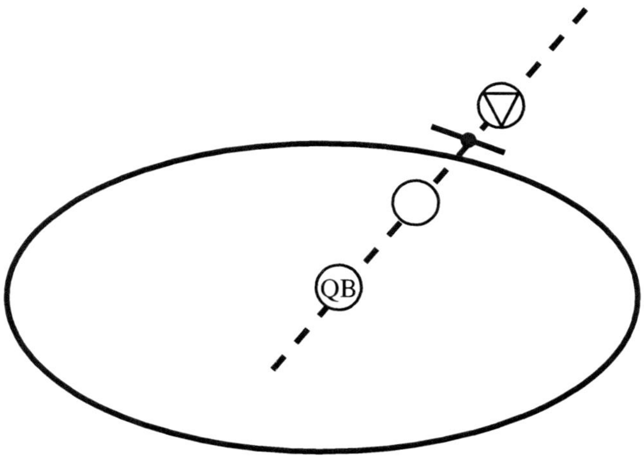

Diagram #3. Cylinder—Pass

It can look like you are oversetting, but you have to understand the center of the cylinder. I am not going past my junction point because I am going to go fast to that point, slow down just for a second, which might be imperceptible, and then I am going to jump you and then get ready to redirect.

Angles of Approach

- Junction point
- Width of the defender
- Angle of his backbone
- Stance—Inside hand or outside hand?

The width of the defender determines the junction point. The angle of his backbone also determines it. If his inside hand is down, he can make a quick move to the inside. If his outside hand is down, he cannot.

Daily Drill Menu

- Over the line
- Around the square
- Patty cake
- Hop-hop
- Down the line
- Pressure wave

Let me go over some drills with you. The over the line is just a drill where we line up on the line, set hut, they turn and open their hips to the right or left at 90 degrees and take a few steps as they straddle the line. It isn't fast; they haven't even warmed up yet. You have to do something to get the hips opened up, and then your foot will go. The object is to keep the hips down. We describe it as keeping your belt buckle down. You would use this when pulling, for pass protection, and cutting off. I go twice to the left and twice to the right before practice even starts.

Around the square is just shuffling the feet along a square. We set out cones at about 3x3'. I want to hear the feet. The object is to stay flat-footed.

We already talked about patty cake. Creep, and reduce distance. Creep is just taking little bitty baby steps to get into the junction point. Get to him before he gets to you. Shake hands.

We have a hop drill. We start in a fitted position with the offensive player chopping his feet. The defender has his weight into the blocker and at the snap brings his momentum forward. We want the blocker to actively resist under control, like a power clean. Hop and absorb his force. Get your butt down get smaller, and then hop back against his resistance. Then, you can redirect him whichever direction he wants to go.

With down the line, you want to snap your hands and rip. Wax on/wax off, hand slap. Hop hop, follow your hands, butt and jerk. Always replace your hands. When you put up your hands, flip them back around. That way if a defender goes to slap your hands, you have flipped them so he misses, and then you have replaced them. You are not trying to thump him with your hands.

We practice our spin move. The blocker engages the defender, who moves in one direction and then spins back to the other direction. The blocker should spin with his back to the defender and then reengage right in front of him. We run these drills at a slower speed and then we do it live as well.

With the pressure wave, we are just forcing the guy to relocate and change direction along the dish. The defender can go to either side, hand slap, or whatever. We want to lag slightly behind but keep redirecting along the dish maybe four or five times. It doesn't really happen as frequently in a true pass rush, but we drill it that way. I would take this drill and patty cake, and go out and teach pass protection if I could just have two drills.

To recap, the stuff that I teach I know works. It is natural movements and not robotic. Use little bitty baby steps to creep with your toe out and play the game with your feet. This should be just like any other sport. Pass protection is just like guarding the basket. Lag behind him, and run the dribbler out of bounds.

When I got into coaching and scouting players, I called up Tiger Johnson and asked him what he looked for in an offensive lineman. He said you can take all of the starting offensive linemen in the NFL and throw them in a bag, shake it up and empty it out and pick any center, two guards, and two tackles and they are all about the same. What truly distinguishes the good ones is character and intelligence. I have never forgotten that, and it is so true.

I want to give you a quote that I believe completely. This is about taking chances and getting away from the valley of darkness and all of that:

> *If you treat him as if he were what he ought to be and could be, he will become what he ought to be and could be.*
>
> —Johann Wolfgang von Goethe

This is really appropriate for football. You are trying to raise their individual levels of play a little higher than what everybody else thinks they are going to play at for you. If they can play at that level and the rest of the team can count on them, you have done something. I would wish that for all of you. Coaching has been an incredible reward for me personally. Do a few things; do them extraordinarily well!

ABOUT THE AUTHOR

Howard Mudd is a veteran offensive line coach of the National Football League and a former offensive lineman in the NFL. From 1998 to 2009, he was the offensive line coach for the Indianapolis Colts, with whom he won Super Bowl XLI. He played seven seasons for the San Francisco 49ers and the Chicago Bears from 1964 to 1970 in the National Football League. Mudd was a three-time Pro Bowler in 1966, 1967, and 1968. He retired in 1971 due to a knee injury, and began his coaching career at the University of California the following year.

Mudd pursued a coaching career following his retirement as an NFL player. He spent two years as an assistant coach at the University of California, before moving to the NFL, and coaching for the San Diego Chargers, San Francisco 49ers, Seattle Seahawks, Cleveland Browns, and Kansas City Chiefs between 1974 and 1997.

He then joined the Indianapolis Colts as an offensive line coach, where he coached from 1998 to 2009. During his 12 years in Indianapolis, the Colts allowed the fewest sacks in the NFL, with just 218 sacks in 182 games. This is especially impressive when the high number of passing plays the Colts attempted during that time period was taken into account. Peyton Manning played for the Colts for 11 of those 12 years, and credits much of his success to the protection he's received from Mudd's front line.

On May 6, 2009, ESPN reported that Mudd had filed his retirement papers due to a change in the NFL's pension program. On May 20, 2009, Mudd returned to the team as the senior offensive line coach. Mudd planned to retire for good following the Colts' game against the New Orleans Saints in Super Bowl XLIV.

In May 2010, Mudd and New Orleans Saints offensive line coach Aaron Kromer were together for a coaching clinic in Cincinnati, at which time Kromer approached Mudd about serving as a temporary consultant with the Saints. Mudd first advised the Saints during the 2010 off-season, then returned for the opening of training camp. In reference to his association with the Saints, Mudd said, "He [Kromer] asked me to come down and spend a little time, and I said, 'Okay.' I'll only be here a couple of days. That's it."

Mudd was named the offensive line coach for the Philadelphia Eagles after being talked out of retirement on February 2, 2011. In Mudd's first season with the Eagles, they allowed 17 fewer sacks than they had the previous season, and helped LeSean McCoy lead the NFL in total touchdowns.

Scott Peters

PUNCHING, STOPPING THE BULL RUSH, AND LONG-ARM RUSHING

Safe Football LLC—Hand Combat Specialist

Thank you, Coach McNally. I appreciate those kind words. I did not expect to speak, but it looks as if it is going to happen. I want to share some views with you after hearing all of the other great presenters before me. There has been a lot of information exchanged, and I want to get specific about a few things. Hopefully, these things will be of help to you.

One of the points I want to talk about is to minimize exposure. Last week, we watched a lot of film out in Arizona. I noticed a lot of the players today are keeping their hands wide.

I do not want to beat a dead horse, and we have all heard the analogy, but I will bring that back into play because I think there are a lot of parallels there, especially where you want to carry your hands. There is a reason for that. You can say the chest is to football what the chin is to boxing. I see offensive players letting their chest be a doormat for defenders. I do not like this at all. I feel we should be doing more to protect our chest.

I am going to discuss minimizing exposure and maximizing the damage we can inflict. Coach Howard Mudd just spoke on being aggressive on pass protection, and I am a fan of that aspect of the game. We want to disrupt the feet of the defenders. Coach McNally talked about playing long, and those things will come into play here today. We are going to get into the angle A set for a short period of time. I want to cover a couple of things that I hope will help the offensive players.

Limiting options is a theoretical thing, real briefly I do not plan on getting too theoretical. We will talk about it briefly.

We see blockers getting wider with their hands. It is no fun getting split down the middle. We do not want the sternum to collapse, and we want to prevent that from happening. We are going to do some things to minimize that from happening.

We see too many offensive players taking options off the table. I talk with players that are saying, "Shoot, I can't win." I want players to know the defenders can defeat them to the inside, outside, or down the middle. If we can teach players where they are vulnerable, that is a big advantage for the blocker.

If we look at an offensive guard blocking on a 3-technique defender, we can review his thoughts. He may try to square up on the 3 technique. He may be concerned what he will do if the defender goes inside or outside. What will he do if the defender comes into the chest of the guard? So the guard has three concerns he is aware of and is not sure what he will do on the three options he has given the defender.

This is how I explain the best thing for the guard to do. I will explain it in these terms. If you have to protect your house, what are you going to do? You have two doors in the house. You have some burglar coming in the house. You are standing in the middle of the house with your gun. You hear something, and you are freaking out. Your head is on a swivel, and you are subject to anything that comes your way. You are in a state of paranoia.

You go to one of the doors and sit down. You aim the gun at the other door. Now you are protecting the door where you are sitting, and you are only vulnerable at the door where you have the gun pointing. Therefore, you can protect that door better. That is just a mentality, if this works for you.

The point is the fact that you can take things off the table. What do I mean by that statement? It means by getting somebody, presence helps. For example if I am a guard and I am facing a 3 technique, we know we are vulnerable to the inside. We can take that inside move away from the defender. This means we can dictate what the defender is going to do by giving him the path of least resistance. That path would be to the outside.

I want to make sure my inside arm post is strong. Getting the inside arm up where it is more of a weapon for me will encourage the defender to go outside.

We want to discourage defenders on certain moves by taking away their options. I will discuss some of those options later. I have a punch that is very powerful that I will talk about. It has been successful for those people that have been trained to use it, and they have agreed that it is powerful. That technique is called the "pillar."

We are about disruption. We want to disrupt defenders' feet. We will talk about angle A as Coach McNally discussed earlier. After being a skeptic of that technique, I am now convinced it is a technique we should use. I want to show a couple of demonstrations on that technique.

We are going to get into the bull rush and how we can defend that move and how to discourage that technique. This is a big concern, and we want to discourage that move, but we know we are going to see more and more of that technique by the defense, especially when the blocker is opening up his chest area.

How many of you have a problem with the long-arm pass rush? There is a problem with the long-arm rush, and if you watch enough film, you will notice. I will cover a few points on this technique so you can give some options to your players.

The next area I want to cover relates to the drop-post. Coach McNally touched on this briefly. I know it seems a little backward in thinking. Everyone talks about when we are post setting the inside man always sets into the line of scrimmage.

This is a habit, and it is something we have always done. This makes sense if you can do that. Realistically, when the defense is gaining the edge, you have to drop-step. I want to show you a couple of points for that move, and it is very powerful. It is counterintuitive to what we have all been taught and what we have always heard for a long time.

At the end, I have a couple of drills I want to show you. So this is what we want to do here today.

I want to bring up the assistant line coach for the University of Cincinnati to help with the demonstrations: Coach Ryan Pugh.

The first thing I want to do is to get real clear about my hands. I want to discuss what I call "on guard." Last night, Blaise Winter discussed how a boxer wants to keep his hands in front of the face to protect his head. As an offensive lineman, I like to carry my hands just under my chin. I call that position "guard". I have my elbows tight and my thumbs are up, and my shoulders are actually rolled forward.

I see some players that have their hands outside their body and just under the armpits.

I see a lot of players that have their hands down near their waist. To me, they are inviting the defenders to go to the chest area.

If you take a look at most careers in football, and I do not know the reason behind this theory, but I do not think most football players trust their feet. It may be that they have not developed their hands and have kept their hands in tight. It does not cost them anything to protect themselves. I think it is important that we do that.

If you take a look at most careers in football, and I do not know the reason behind this theory, but I do not think most football players trust their feet. It may be that they have not developed their hands and have kept their hands in tight. It does not cost them anything to protect themselves. I think it is important that we do that.

Back to the boxing analogy, players that use their chin as a setup tool do not have a long career. Take Muhammad Ali, for example. He set up his opponents with his own chin. We do not want to do that. I know this is football, but I want to reference that point.

In our guard position, our hands are up and the thumbs are up. We have our hands just below the chin. Our elbows are bent. We are nice and relaxed. We want to have our hands nice and loose. We say elbows tight, but we do not carry our elbows against our body. We simply wring them out, and bring them up in front of the chest.

From this position, I can deliver, I can attack, and I can counter, and do all of that, and I am loose. If one of the arms gets knocked down, it is not the end of the world. I am not in bad shape. Again, my shoulders are forward, and I can deliver a lot of power behind my strike. That is what I call my guard position. The best thing about this is the fact you have your hands up and you can deliver from this position, and you are nice and loose.

I want to talk about disrupting the footwork of the defender. We use a very quick inside stab on the move. Let's say I am the left guard, and Coach Pugh is a 3 technique. You will notice that the good defenders are not going to give you their chest. Some offensive players are still throwing big haymakers down the pike. What happens is the blockers get caught off balance with their hands too far out front and their butts up. This is one of the reasons many players have gone away from throwing hands.

The thing about the pillar is the fact that it is fully extended. In this case, it is my right arm. I have my thumbs up. Coach McNally brought up my bench press. Yes, I can tell you I benched a lot. But I can tell you this: there is no correlation of your strength and what you do on the football field with your strength. There may be some aspects that are connected, but that is a big tipping point. When you get where you can bench press a lot, you get to the point where you lose some function. You can't even touch your elbows together. That was the way it was for me. If I cannot touch my elbows together, I have done a couple of things that hinder my ability to block. If my elbows are flaring out, my kinetic energy level goes out the back of my elbows, and I lose a lot of power there. It forces my thumbs inside, and there is always the tendency to lean forward when that happens. If my elbows are inside, it helps keep my back straight.

We do a lot more of the straight bar bench presses. We are also doing some of the hand movement exercises in the off-season. I think this is an epidemic, and we are seeing this from more players.

I watch enough tapes, and I see players getting blown up. They have their hands outside, or down low with their palms down. The position of the hands in front of the chest with the thumbs up is common position we see in a lot of martial arts experts.

It is about extension and length. Your power is not derived from the press. It is from the speed and the lockout and to the extension using the subscapular. The arm is locked out by the time the defender runs into it. I call this "running into the post." If the defender uses his chest and runs into my post, which is a one-arm extension, I am going to have a degree of whiplash from the collision. That is a not a huge investment on my part to do that.

I want to show you how this works. I set in my position with my hands in front of my chest. I have my thumbs up. As the defender comes toward me, I use my one arm and hand. It is a real quick move. As the hand makes contact, I turn the thumb outside slightly before contact.

It is easy for me to extend the right arm. It is a jab with the right arm. The left arm and hands remain in front of my chest. I use the extended arm as a pillar. As the defender comes forward, I jab and reset my feet. Again, I jab and reset my feet. This is not a lot of effort. It is just enough to pop the defender's feet and force him to reset. It is really disruptive for the defender.

I am going to have Coach McNally be the rusher? Okay! As he comes toward me, my arm is almost locked out. Also, the hips are locked. As he comes hard toward me, I reset my feet and use the pillar again. I still have my thumbs up, and I am only using the one pillar on the technique. It is not a lot of effort, but enough to pop his feet.

Coach McNally: When I first saw this technique, I did not understand it. But when I started doing the technique, I realized what was happening. As I lock my arm and make contact, I also lock my hip. That makes a great deal of difference.

Scott Peters: My kick leg is going to be involved in this as well. I am not leaning forward. That is a problem for most guys that throw punches. I have some extension in my back hip and my kick leg. When I make contact with the hand on the defender's shoulder, I am not leaning forward. My hips stay engaged, and my lower back is tight. It is boom! Reset, and boom again. I have not invested a great deal of energy here. It is easy. It does take repetition in getting used to the technique.

I will teach you a drill instructing players on how to do the technique. It is a wired coordination drill. It is another fighting arts tool. The extension of the punch is not just with the arm extended. It is the extra short distance that makes the pop that gets the defender knocked out. As the hand makes contact, it gets an extra snap from the arm at the last six inches. It is the subscapular pop that you get at the end of the extension that makes the difference.

The drill we are using to develop this punch is called subscapular push-ups. The best way I know how to tell people how to do the drill is to show them. As I go down to a push-up position, my elbows do not bend. My arms are at shoulder-width. My thumbs are up. I am trying to touch my shoulder blades together.

Let's go back to the pillar on the defender. I make contact and step into the man making contact with the one arm extended. As I come forward and make contact, look at the power I have in my legs. I have some power in the upper body. You can stop the defender's feet with this move.

Most of you may have seen the timing drill. This is a finished position. I am starting with my elbows already locked. I find this drill is a good way for players to understand the move. They need to know their range, and they need to know what it feels like at the end of the drill. This allows them to work backward and really know what to do on the drill.

I have both hands up with the arms locked out. The defender comes in with his shoulders exposed. As the defender comes forward, I want to use both hands and make contact as the defender comes forward. The contact is enough to stop the feet of the defender.

We want to be in a position where we do not compromise our balance, but we want to deliver a strong blow on the technique. By keeping our hands inside, we can gain enough power without compromising our balance.

Do we have any questions on what we have covered at this point?

Question: Are there other exercises we can use to teach the push-ups to develop the post scapular technique? What about doing work with dumbbells?

You can do dips to develop the technique. If you are doing bench press exercises with the thumbs up, that is better than using dumbbells. We do not want to use anything that is contrary to what we are doing with the push-ups.

The one-arm technique is considered a single post. I have talked about this aspect of the block at this point. Everyone is going for the chest area. I do not want to do that because I do not know what I am going to get when I am in a stance. I do know what is available to me for the most part, when I am in my stance, and that is the big pad on the defender's shoulder. If I can find that spot, I can get the job done.

I am not trying to de-cleat the man. I am not trying for a home run. I know the shoulder area is going to be there for me. I want to disrupt his feet a little. It does not take a lot of effort to do this. I know this will slow him down. It is working for me and it seems to be a simple tool for the offensive lineman.

As the defender makes his move, I want to get the right hand on the left shoulder of the defender. Now, I know it is not over at this point. I still have my left hand up. The other hand can be a bait hand if it is up high.

We know a lot of defenders are trying to chop that left arm down on the blocker. As I said before, we are taking things off the table that the defense has to attack the blocker. As the defender brings his right hand over to chop the blocker's left hand, he makes an inside move with the left hand and gets it on the right shoulder and inside the arm of the defender. He may have to refit the hand as the defender knocks the arm down.

This is a very effective way to block the man. It is a very conservative way to block the defender, and it takes some skill, and it takes time to master this technique.

Coach McNally talked about the move inside by the defender. As the defender tries to go inside, I have to punch with the right hand and reset and hop back with my feet to get the extension I need.

I want to keep my feet in a balanced position. That jab is very powerful. Offensive players lose power when they roll their hips forward. They need to lock the hips and stay upright and keep their feet in position to move backward as they reset the hands on each move.

The hip is extremely powerful. That is where the strength comes from on this technique. As the defender tries to come inside, I slide in that direction and jab with the inside hand. The hip is my power. When the blocker loses power, it is when they get overextended and lose their balance. We want the hips forward, and we want the elbows inside.

The punch on the inside move against the defender is a chance for us to stop—or at least slow down—the defenders. We stop his feet momentarily to prevent him from running through us. In talking about the use of the arms as a pillar, you can use the technique with either arm. I think the technique is very effective.

Moving on, I want to talk about the angle A block real quick. I am blocking against a wide defender. I move my feet as I kick outside. I move down the line toward the defender. I make contact with my near hand on the shoulder once, and then a second time. I want to slow him down.

Then, I come with the offside arm and punch him on the inside top of his shoulder. We are touching him, and we are not trying to knock him off his feet.

We want to keep our shoulders square throughout the block. I want to stay square to the line of scrimmage. As I move down the line, I make contact on the near shoulder of the defender. I slide and make contact with the near pillar one or two times. Then, I come across with the offside pillar at the top of the shoulder to break the momentum of the defender.

We are making enough contact to disrupt the defender's movement off the ball. The defender is not the same threat as he would be if he was able to get three steps up the field before contact. I want to stay in an inside-out position so the defender cannot change directions and come inside on me.

If a player has short arms and does not feel this technique will work for him, there are other ways to do it. I have seen some players that have short arms but were very good with their hands. It depends a great deal on how the player carries his hands, and how quickly he can get the pillars out to slow down the defender. We are not doing a lot of exertion on the technique.

This technique also works for the tackle position. I move toward the tackle with my hands up. If I can engage the tackle, I can turn him. I do not like to talk about turning, but if we get a wide rusher turned up, we walk him upfield.

If we engage the defender inside, we can turn him. I do not like to talk about turning, but the width has a lot to do with the distance I have to cover to get to the defender. Again, we are talking about a wide rusher. We like to teach the block with the offensive man square as possible.

We see a lot of blockers that kick, and kick for three kicks, and they end up turning their shoulders and their chest is open to the defender, and then they are done.

As we kick outside, we have our hands up in position to strike the defender as we get near him. My thumb is on the inside when I use my opposite hand arm to strike the top of the shoulder of the defender. It is a one-two punch on the inside shoulder of the defender. First is the inside arm, and second is the outside arm. It is the left arm, and then the right arm.

On the first initial strike, I am not going to grab the shoulder pad and try to lift the blocker. That is not ideal. I am going to reset the hand and work for a better position. By striking the defender, I have made it more difficult for him to attack me upfield because of the speed with which the block takes place.

I come with the left hand on his left shoulder, and then my right hand comes on the top of the shoulder of the defender with my thumb turned inside. The first punch comes across my body, and the second punch comes straight from the right hand and can be very effective. It is left hand, reset, and then the right hand. Left boom, reset, right boom!

The right hand fits nicely on the left shoulder of the defender. The left hand is a slight disruption for the defender. The right hand is the more powerful punch. As Coach McNally said, we are not trying to grab the defender as much as we are trying to stun him and then to reset.

I am all for grabbing. I am not saying we are going to hit defenders and then let them go back. This is a situation of whatever is available from the defense.

If a defender's chest plate is open, we will pursue that position. If his chest area is open, I am going to lock the defender up with both hands under his front pads. I want to tighten my elbows down, screw my thumbs out, and get my fingers under the pads. I can do what I have to do from there. We have taken the advantage away from the defender right off the snap.

The defender is going full speed, and that technique may be difficult. There are other opportunities as I mentioned.

Coach McNally: It is interesting to me to see how quickly Scott Peters gets his hands back on the defenders. He does not hold his hands away from his body at all. His arms are slightly extended, and the punch comes with a quick move with the hips locking out as the hand makes contact with the defender.

Scott Peters: I do not pull the arms back to the point my elbows are bent. I am keeping the hands in a position in front of my chest. Some of the defenders try different things to confuse the blocking lineman. Some defenders will stutter step to try to screw up the timing of the blockers.

If I can keep my hands up in front of my chest, I do not have to move the hands far to make contact on the defender's shoulder. The punch is real strong, and it is powerful. It all relates to mechanics instead of trying to hit the defender harder. It is mechanics, and it comes from the subscapular.

The first step you want to accomplish is to protect yourself. This is always good. If you get in a fight, the guy that drops his hands is the guy that gets knocked out. You may have a great haymaker, but you are not going to make it in boxing unless you have a good defense.

Next, I want to discuss stopping the bull rush cuff technique. I have a drill tape where I discuss five techniques to stop a bull rush. It should be in the included in the drills that the COOL Clinic has for sale. I want to show you one of those techniques today. It is very simple, but it is effective. It is the one bull rush everyone should know.

If I have made contact and the defender is pushing me back, I do not take my hands off the top of the defender's pads. I call this technique the cuff. The defender has his hands on my chest and is pushing me back. I have my hands on top of his arms and on the top of his pads.

It is almost as if the pads are a lever. I snap my elbows down on the arms of the defender. I take a hop back as I exert the elbows down on his arms, and as I hop back, his momentum pulls him down in front of me. I hop, and the defender is on the ground. It is very simple. It is not a trap because I do not disconnect my hands.

All I am doing is to snap my hands down. It is just my wrist coming down with my elbows bent against his arms. The distance he has to jump back is a big factor for the defender to overcome. It is not a hop back that we use because we do not sway the back. Our elbows do hit the defender's arms. However, it is a matter of stopping the hips as we come back. You look down as your feet hit the ground.

The jersey on top of the shoulder pad can act as a handle for you as you should not have to rise up too much as you get better at it. All you are trying to do is to get the defender into a position where we can use our hands to pull him down.

We have other techniques that are simple and easy to execute. I like to have a variety of techniques to use because you never know who you are going to be dealing with.

Step one is the defense we use against the wide defender. Step two is to discourage the defender from ever trying it again. On the long arm technique, we want to get our arm inside the defender's arm. Step one is to never let the defender get his arm into your chest. Step two is to circle outside the defender's arm and bring it back underneath the defender.

I do not want to raise my arm high on the movement from the top of the arm to the area underneath his arm. I simply raise my hand, and slide the hand back underneath the defensive man. I am not going to alter my position by making a big circle with the arm. Again, we are just raising the center of gravity with my hips.

If I have to hop back on the defender, I will. I do not want to hop back, but if I do, I do not want to sway my back and lose my balance. You must be careful on this drill because you can dislocate the arm of the defender on the maneuver.

Another thing we can do is to grab the top of the defender's pad and turn him inside. I use the top of the shoulder pad as a handle and drop him down by applying force on the top of his shoulder.

If the defender has his hand in the middle of my chest, I can still long-arm him. I may bring my chin down to steady his arm on my chest. When I bring the right hand over the top of the defender's arm and get under his arm, I have control of him.

If the defender is high, I like my chances. I come up underneath his arm and roll his arm outside. Things happen a million miles per hour, but you can start to develop that technique.

I want to get to the different videos of the techniques we have demonstrated today. Do we have any questions on the techniques we have discussed today? Thanks to Coach McNally for having me here today. Thank you for your attention.

ABOUT THE AUTHOR

Former Arizona Cardinals player Scott Peters is on a quest, developing a nonprofit business that makes football safer for professional and young athletes.

Safe Football LLC was launched by the 35-year-old Peters, who said he had a history of concussions throughout his professional and college playing days, including one sustained without any helmet contact.

Because there is no helmet that will resolve the injury issue and the safest football involves simply not playing, Peters is out to show the techniques he developed that he believes will make the sport safer by using a combination of mixed martial arts and biomechanics.

"It's about achieving vertical lift with the hands instead of horizontal contact," said Peters, who holds a communications bachelor's degree from Arizona State University. "It allows someone smaller to overpower someone larger, using tapping and lifting techniques. It takes away their power. You're operating with perfect alignment and compromising their spine and shoulder movements. It's as safe as it's going to get."

With approximately 3 million youth playing football, and a major push by colleges and the NFL to implement various efforts to reduce concussions, the nonprofit has a ready-made market for its offerings.

The business is a spinoff of Peters' Fight Ready MMA gym in Scottsdale. The former ASU player set up shop in the Valley and is looking to branch out beyond the fighting skills. "I like to say, 'Save the brain. Save the game,'" said Peters, who sits on concussion analysis panels. "There are better ways to do things."

Peters knows the impact of violent collisions in the game. His after-football career began when he woke up from micro-fracture ankle surgery while playing as an offensive lineman with the Carolina Panthers to discover damaged cartilage that would abruptly end his football career.

Peters retired from the NFL in 2006 at age 27 before getting involved with Brazilian jiu-jitsu training. He's now been practicing and competing for several years and has won two world championships in submission grappling.

His football retirement, however, only lasted a year before the Arizona Cardinals called him. Peters went to Flagstaff for training camp and played well with his new team. He played another two years with the Cardinals, with his final game in Super Bowl XLIII in Tampa, Florida.

During that return to the sport, Peters began to develop different techniques gleaned from his Brazilian jiu-jitsu experience. The idea is to apply leverage using the body's proper stance to generate force, essentially using the arms and hands instead of lunging headfirst into the opposing player.

Coaches and various sports groups are trying to make the sport safer without compromising the game. Peters has said that head safety has been made an issue with many former players suing the NFL about their injuries from concussions.

Peters started training players and eventually began the nonprofit as a comprehensive approach to football. Its goal is to teach younger players techniques to avoid head injuries that can cause brain damage so the game can continue and, ultimately, be even safer.

"I want to get it at every level of football," Peters said.

Dan Cozzetto, a 37-year coach now at the University of Washington, said Grey Ruegamer, one of the co-owners of the business, recently was hired as a full-time strength coach, working specifically with linemen using the techniques Peters taught him. Cozzetto coached both players while at ASU.

Cozzetto says his players use the techniques every day, and so far, there have been no concussions.

"It's made players more aware of how much their hands can become a weapon," said Cozzetto, who commutes and still lives in Ahwatukee. "You've got to learn how to play with your head up."

Al Dahlberg, a Brown University professor of medical science who teaches molecular genetics and medical biochemistry, said he's "delighted" Peters has developed these techniques. As a former high school football player and dad to two former college football players, Dahlberg knows the tough decisions a parent makes on whether to allow their children to play the game.

"It's a tougher game, and neurologists are saying it's difficult to know when a player is really ready to come back to the game after getting a concussion," he said. "These are still relative unknowns. I'm not aware of any successful treatments."

Through his nonprofit, Peters is working with a number of advocacy groups to get the word out and has a long list of endorsements. The goal is to train retired athletes who can then train current players and young athletes. Clinics will begin in March to start teaching younger athletes, and training the trainers is happening now.

"It'll change their lives," Peters said. "Your brain is your operating system. This system is more effective."

DRILLS TO IMPROVE OFFENSIVE LINE PLAY WITH THE RUN AND PASS

NFL Alumni

Is there anyone here that is older than 79? Good! That means I am the oldest guy here. This means I have been around longer than all of you. What is my claim to fame? I am old enough to tell you. I am the coach that came up with the idea of locking out the hands both on the run and the pass block. This came about in 1974. I did not have a guru that I looked up to for advice on the offensive line. I had coached defense all of my life. I was a defensive player. I was an offensive player under the old rule of one-platoon football, and that was because I had to play offense.

When I became an offensive line coach, basically, I coach all of the things I had not done much of before related to the offensive line. I started coaching in 1957. I was a freshman at Penn State. I coached there as a grad assistant, and then a full-time linebacker coach. Then, I came to the University of Cincinnati and coached defense. I was the defensive coordinator.

At Cincinnati, we improved the defense from giving up 32 points a game, to giving up only 9 points per game. Two years later, they gave me the head coaching job. They did not have a contract ready, and two days later I turned down the job. The newspaper the next day had the story on the front page as the headline. "Radakovich Quits Undefeated." That was the only time I was a head coach.

I have been a defensive coach for basically 35 years and an offensive line coach for 15 years. I became the offensive line coach because the Steelers' head coach, Chuck Noll, asked me to do it. I did not apply for the job of offensive line coach. I had coached the defensive line for the Steelers. But at the time, I was out of a job.

I know many of you have heard of the Pittsburgh Steelers "Steel Curtain." They got that name when I was coaching the defensive line for the Steelers. I put that defensive line together. They included Joe Greene, Ernie Holmes, Dwight White, and L.C. Greenwood.

I was down at the Senior Bowl in Mobile. I was out of a job. I had been the offensive coordinator at Colorado for two years and had lost my job. Coach Chuck Noll came up to me and asked me if I would be his offensive line coach. I asked him what he was talking about. He said, "I want you to coach our offensive line."

I asked him what had happened to the offensive line coach, Bob Fry. He said "I fired him." Bob was from Cincinnati, and had played football at the University of Kentucky. Bob was a friend of mine, and I had coached with him two years previously. I agreed to coach the line for Coach Noll, even though I had never been a line coach before.

I did have a background for coaching the offensive line. I had only worked with the offensive line with the freshmen at Penn State one year. Joe Paterno had a quarterback, receiver, and centers camp that summer. That was the first camp for high school kids in America. That camp had started around 1960.

He had me there to coach the centers. Joe Paterno coached the quarterbacks, J.T. White, the ends coach, worked with the receivers. Since I was going to coach the centers, I was not going to have them squat down there and snap the ball to the quarterbacks all day. I had to try to teach them how to block without any pads. At that time, you were not allowed to have pads.

I found two blocking shields, and taught the centers how to hold the shields. Every time they snapped the ball, they had to block the shield off the line for 10 yards, or to knock the person down holding the shield. We went full speed for one hour. We went three times a day for one hour each session.

I worked that camp for four or five years. I even did that for Steve Belichick, who was coaching at the time. He is the father of Bill Belichick, the head coach at New England. George Welsh was on our staff. He was friends with Steve, and he asked me to work their camp. So I worked their camps.

I went to work the camp, and a little kid by the name of Billy wanted to be the center for his high school team. So I coached him for a week, three times a day. I had the centers block the shields, and I even had them block the shields uphill a few times each day. Billy became the starter for his team, and he became the captain of the team. I had 15 centers that I worked with, but Bill was the smallest. However, he was the best center I had to work with. He was a smart kid and learned what we were teaching the centers. He was a smart player then. He always asked good questions.

This is where I learned how to coach players to block the shield dummies. When I was at Penn State, we had the blocking boards and other tools. I did not like those gimmicks. In fact, I hated them.

When I became the offensive line coach for the Steelers, I had to decide how I was going to teach run blocking. I decided I would teach it the same way as I did with those young kids at camp. I wanted the offensive linemen to block the shields 10 yards back, or to knock them on their back. I wanted them to hit the shield dummy and to extend their arms through the block.

The rules at the time stated the offensive lineman blocking had to keep his hands and arms within the framework of the body. You were not allowed to wrap your arms around a defender, ever. The rule did not say if you could extend your hands all the way out or not. It was assumed you could not extend your hands all the way. I got the rule book and I could not find the answer about extending the hands. I decided we would extend the hands on our blocks.

I talked to Chuck Noll about it, and he said, "Fine." Chuck's idea of pass blocking was to butt them with the top of your head, and to extend the arms and punch the defenders in the ribs. Chuck Noll was one hell of a coach, but he did not have all of the answers. From that point on, I taught the Steelers to blow the shields out for 10 yards, to knock the defender on his back.

When I do a drill, from the days I coached the linebackers, I had to make up my own drills because there were not man linebacker coaches. When we were one-platoon, you had to coach both offense and defense. What I am getting at is the fact I had to make up my own drills. I made up my own movement drills, and my own pass protection drills. I had to make up my own linebacker drills. I did not have anyone to copy from.

When I became the offensive line coach, I visited other teams. I went to see the Rams and Coach Chuck Knox. I went to see the 49ers and Dick Stanfield. I knew these coaches, when I was coaching for the Redskins.

I told Coach Noll I wanted to visit the two offensive coaches, Knox and Stanfield. He said, "We do not do that in pro football. We do not go around visiting other teams." I said, "I do!" He said they would not talk to me. I told him if Chuck Knox did not talk to me, I would kick his ass.

I went to the West Coast and saw what they did with their offensive line. I did not like what they did. I did not like either one of them. They did opposites for the twist games. One did the zone against the end tackle, and the other used the man blocking rule against the end tackle defenders. If they faced the tight end, they did just the opposite. They did not do things the same way.

I decided to do my own thing. I made the decision that I would go with my blockers with their hands out, and we would see what happens. We started blocking 1-on-1 with the hands out. It went over great. The defense would grab the shoulder, and the offensive man would push against his arm and grab his jersey and put him on his ass. The basic pass rush was push, pull.

The fact that I had been the defensive line coach two years earlier did not hurt my situation. I knew all of the defensive moves and techniques the defense used.

The first thing we did was to stop the rushers that were not very good. But this was not very good against teams that ran stunts and games against us. A defender would grab us, and we could not switch blocks. I wanted to run the switch like basketball teams used in switching their man-to-man defense. So that is what I did when we started out.

We blew out the shields for 10 yards, or we drove the man to the ground on his back. That was our basic block. We had four basic blocks. We drove straight ahead with the left shoulder and straight ahead with the right shoulder. We blocked down the line right, and down the line left. We executed the reach block to the right, and the reach block to the left. Then, we would block down the line and then spin out. We blocked down, and then we would spin out. Those were our basic blocks.

Next, we went to our double-team blocks. The double-team block and zone block is the same thing. The zone block is a version of the double-team block. Those are our basic blocks.

I did some things differently on our blocks. You will see these points covered in the double-team drill. Some teams have the outside arm free, and they pump the arm back and forth as they drive the defender back. I do not use the swinging of the arm technique. I want the blocker to use the forearm. I try to hand the defender we are working the double-team block against, and have one of the blockers move on up to the next defender, which would be the linebacker.

I have two people that will assist me with the demonstrations. I have Andrew Richardson, who played for Penn State. His senior year, he was the starting right tackle. They won the Big 10 Championship in 2005. Also, I have Colyn Haugh, who was a defensive tackle for us at Robert Morris University. He is very short, and his nickname was "Plug." The year he was a senior, he was the best defensive lineman we had. We were ranked first in four categories on defense in Division AA at Robert Morris University. He was quick as a cat.

Drew Richardson is now the offensive line coach at Robert Morris University, and Colyn Haugh is the new offensive line coach at Westminster College. He is just learning defensive football. All he has worked on are some drills in the racquetball court with me. We are going to demonstrate the four basic blocks today.

After we complete these demonstrations, I have a film to show that will include the blocking techniques, and you will see some of the work by the Steelers in 1974. That is when I was just starting to coach.

The only other thing I want to tell you is this: today is only about the fifth clinic I have done in my life. When I became a line coach, right away we went to two Super Bowls. We developed the best pass protection in the league. We had a good run blocking scheme as well. We had the most yards in 1974 in the AFC Division. Dallas had 36 more yards than we had, and they were in the NFC. However, they did not make the playoffs. The next year, we were third in the most yards gained. O.J. Simpson was playing for Buffalo, and we ended up third in yards gained in 1975. Still, we were pretty damn good.

BASE RUN DRILLS AND BLOCKS

Right Shoulder Block

The blocker is going to get off as low as he can. He is going to hit with the right shoulder and right forearm. We want to make contact and move the defender as much as possible. Then, we want to follow through after the contact. We want to accelerate the feet and drive the defender back.

We want both hands in the chest area of the defender. One hand should be in the center of the chest, and the other hand should be under the armpit of the defender. Placement of the hands is very important. You must sink when you block. No matter how good of a blocker you are, sometimes the hands are going to get out of place.

You have to regroup during the block. Even if you have used this technique for 10 years, there will be times when things are not perfect. You will need to regroup. You must be able to think.

I am emphatic on how you hold the dummy shield. One time, I was trying to show Coach Mike Barry how to hold the shield. He was embarrassed that I was telling him how to hold the shield. "I know how to hold the shield." Well, let me tell you there is a way to hold the shield.

The way you hold the shield is to give the most resistance you can humanly give. There is only one way to do that, and that is the way we do it. The player or person holding the shield is going to hold the shield with his left hand in the straps on the back of the shield. Then, he puts his right shoulder behind the shield and positions his bent arm under the shield.

The person holding the shield has the same foot and leg forward as the blocker. He wants to hit the blocker with the shield in that position as the blocker comes off the snap count.

The blocker comes off the line and makes contact on the right shoulder of the defender. He positions his hands with one hand in front of the chest, and one arm under the defender's armpit. He wants to drive the dummy straight back off the line of scrimmage.

It is all one block when we are going straight ahead. We are going to one side or the other on the defender. I never go head-to-head, against the defender. Heads-on is easy. All you do is to stick your hands out with your arms as wide as your shoulders.

As the blocker comes off the ball and hits, he is going straight back or to the blocker's right. We blow the defender back in the direction we want him to go.

I do not believe in short, choppy steps, or "little feet," or anything like that. I believe in accelerating your ass off, as hard as you can. I believe in doing it, and doing it until you get coordinated at doing it. The faster you drive the defender back, the larger steps you are going to take. We have film to show you that this works.

In zone blocking, the offensive player may end up crossing his feet. I do not believe in a "board" to help the blocker to keep his feet spread as he drives the defender back. I want the blocker to hit the defender as hard as he can, and then drive him back like he is running a 100-yard dash. We want to blow him right through the end zone. We run this drill full speed, with or without pads. As you see, the hands come right through the defender.

How many of you here today teach the block with the thumbs up? Okay! I would fire you all if you were coaching for me. We know from the lecture by Blaise Winter that it is more powerful to block with the thumbs inside than to have the thumbs up. I can assure you it is much stronger with the thumbs inside, and not pointing up.

I coached Joe Greene, L.C. Greenwood, and all of the Steel Curtain players. We had to practice against those players. There was no way I was going to try to block Joe Greene with my thumbs up. If I can hit the defender in the chest area with both hands with the thumbs inside, I can control the defender better. If I can slide one hand to the defender's armpit, it helps with controlling the defender. You will see how this helps on pass protection.

Let me move on to the left shoulder block. The left hand is in the middle of the defender. The right hand is under the armpit. The skill is this: we hit with the shoulder and extend the arms with the elbows inside and the hands in the chest of the defender.

It is boom, boom! It is a simple skill, but it takes kids forever to learn how to do it. It takes some players until their third or fourth year to learn this technique. Some players never learn the technique.

Question: Where are the hands on contact with the defender?

If we are blocking with the right shoulder, we come off the ball with the right arm bent at the elbow where we can make contact in the chest area. Then, we bring the left hand up and under the defender's armpit. Then we drive the defender back for 10 yards if possible. It is two woos. Woo-woo! I want to emphasize the fact we want to hit the defender hard enough to get him started back. The moment contact is made, we want to accelerate the feet, and go like hell.

We do not worry about steps. We are not that concerned with how big the steps are. We step (or heel) to the side we are going to. When I say heel, it means the weight is going to the side we are going to.

That is the base block. Next is the down block. We are going to look at the down block to the right. Now we are going to hit the defender in the chest with both hands and bring both hands up under the armpits and blow the man back off the line of scrimmage.

What is important on a down block? The first point on the down block is not to step inside. We do not want to step up. The important thing is to step at the defender, or just to "heel" it. Make contact, accelerate the feet, and drive the defender back. The better you are these techniques, the less you are going to go heads up with the defender in a game.

Down-the-Line Block

If you can go with a down block with the near shoulder, and we always go with the near shoulder, it helps. However, there are some plays where penetration may hurt. If you cannot hit the defender with the near shoulder, and you penetrate, you end up with your head in front of the defender. This is a judgment you must make. You have to make that decision to use the near shoulder or to use the head-in-front technique to block the defender. We always go head and shoulder, unless we have figured out it is better to lead with the head in front.

Our blocks are always marked at 10 yards. When we have scrimmages or drills, I do not have to tell the blockers to block them farther. They know in all drills we block the defender for 10 yards. They get in the habit of going 10 yards. We always go full speed.

Reach Block

Our next block is the reach block. We are going to demonstrate the reach block. We are going to reach block the man on our right shoulder. We want to use the right shoulder to make the initial contact. The blocker puts his hand down where his foot is. Why? We do not want the blocker to parallel reach. We want him to turn the whole way. It is a hard reach block. We want the body of the blocker to turn. The blocker takes a crossover step, a turn with the outside foot, and then he tries to turn the defender away from the direction he is lined up in.

One line coach I was working with came to me and said, "Do you know what that crazy coach is doing?" That was Coach Tony Wise. The other guy was trying to get the blocker to step to the outside of the defender and block him away from the play. You never do that in a game. In the game, you have a blocker on the outside, blocking down on the man, and the backside blocker is always reaching. He is reaching to close the seam between his outside and the inside of the blocker working with him.

Spin Out Block

This is my favorite block. This is the fourth basic block. He is going to block down and the defender is going to spin out on him. I told you I did not believe in wide feet, or anything like that. In this block, when the defender starts to spin out, you have to widen your feet. You have to feel it, and you widen as you change directions. As the blocker spins out, my head is coming up, and I am using my hands to keep contact with the defender. I want to catch him with my hands as he spins out, and then I want to drive him down the line. The blocker must shuffle his feet as the defender makes his spin. He may spin more than once.

Those are our basic 1-on-1 drills which we do every day after the warm-up session. For us, the warm-up is stance and starts. All we do in stance and starts is to go straight ahead right foot, straight ahead left foot. We go 45 degrees to the left and go down the line and 45 degrees to the right and go down the line. We go straight down the line, straight down the line again. Then we pull at the backward angle each way. Then, we do pass sets. That is what we do on stance and starts so we do not have to waste time on that drill.

Double-Teams

I need two volunteers to assist us. You will be blown out of here. We need you to hold the shield and to be blown out on the double-team blocks. Here we go! We have two young volunteers.

This is a very big disagreement I have with the techniques used by other coaches. I really get upset on this disagreement because I do not believe in pumping the outside arm (or the free arm) while double-teaming with another blocker.

I want to hit as low as I can with my left arm going into the chest of the defender. My right hand goes under his armpit. It is whoop, whoop, and blow him out and try to put him on his neck. We try to put him on his neck.

With zone blocking with the linebacker at the next level, and it does not matter where you put him, the blocker going up to the linebacker pushes off the double-team block. He does not pump. He pushes off with both hands.

Most of you have heard of Coach Joe Moore. He is no longer living. He coached at the University of Pittsburgh several years. Later, he went to work with Lou Holtz and Notre Dame. I went to see him, and he was doing the double-team drill with the one player working that outside arm, and they drove the defender back. Both blockers were working the off hand, before they came off on the linebacker.

I went up to Joe and said, "Joe, what the hell are you doing? You should be pushing the defender with both hands." He replied, "If I do that, my guys will not get to the linebacker. They will just stay with the defensive linemen they are double-teaming."

I said, "Bullcrap! Are you saying you are not good enough as a coach to teach the players to put two hands on the defender and still get one of them to come off on the linebacker? If you can't teach that technique, you should not be coaching the offensive line."

You can still be pushing the man you are working against and then come off on the linebacker. Rich Saul was the best at it. My punter was Dan Ryczek. He weighed 220 pounds, and he punted for me. I did not have a punter for three games. Lucky for us, we did not play anyone that could compete with us. We played three poor teams. Rick Saul only weighed 240 pounds. He was quick as a cat. He would hold the man up for Dan Ryczek, and then Rick Saul would go and cut the linebacker.

We won three straight games, and then we played Dallas. They played a 4-3 defense. Ryczek got killed against their defense.

We are going to work against the defensive down man and the linebacker. First, we are going to look at the block on the down lineman. This is a forehand double-team block. If you can stand up to a two-man forehand double-team, you are better than any nose man that ever lived.

The best defensive man we faced was Curley Culp, who played for Kansas City and Detroit. He was the best in the world against the double-team block. We would double-team block him, but we did not come off on the linebacker. We used a special lead play, where the guard came around the center and took the linebacker that lined over him. We let Rocky Bleier handle the load block. Frankie went for two 80-yard runs, and we kicked the crap out of them.

Curley would get on the double-team block on his back with his feet up in the air. The blockers would have him four feet off the ground, and he would stick his feet up in the air. I wanted to find a picture of that block for my book, but never could find the photo.

This is the forehand double-team block. All double-team blocks should be forehand double-teams. We have heard about the point of getting the hips of the two blockers together. You close the seams of the double-team block with your shoulder. They do not have to be together. Close with the shoulders. Then you oomph, oomph, and drive the man back 10 yards. We should be able to pick him up and throw him on his ass. That is the base.

If the nose man is in a cocked position or tilted, and you are double-teaming him, it is a little different. You cannot go shoulder to shoulder. Joe Greene will split that block. The center has to hook block on the nose man. He has to close the seam with the guard when you are double-teaming a cocked nose man.

You can do all of your blocks with this technique. You can run your trap plays and double-team blocks. You can go full speed on these drills.

For run blocking, you block the way we just covered with a shield against the defenders, where we get between the defender and the ballcarrier. You can chip off the block, which we call a cheap double-team block.

We had a play with the Steelers that we called "special." We faked the trap sweep. When the defensive end closed down, he got cut, and the guard and the back went out and around him. They got the outside linebacker and the play went for good yardage.

On that play, it was important to get between the linebacker and the noseguard with our tackle. He had to make sure he was between the defender and the ballcarrier going wide. You did not need movement on the defenders. So we used the chip technique on the double-team block for that play.

Chip Block

On the chip block, we still have the double-team block. After the outside blocker makes contact and has the down lineman going backward, he chips off to the linebacker. He must make sure he is on the side of the linebacker, where he is between the ballcarrier and the linebacker. He makes sure he walls the linebacker off. Movement is not necessary, but he needs to wall him off from the ballcarrier.

There is one other thing I want to discuss. You can cut defenders in the open field. Since you can cut, we need a cut drill. When I was at Penn State, I invented mat tackling. I do not believe in picking up the offensive man and then driving him on the ground.

We took a light dummy, and we used the same dummy we used to block punts on. We had a player hold up the dummy from the side. The guard would come at the dummy and drive through the dummy low with his shoulder. He could use the right or the left shoulder. He simulated going at a defender to cut him at his knees.

When working on a drill to block punts, when we hit the dummy it would spin back toward the punter. The thing about the cut block is that you must give them a rule when to cut the defender. Our rule was to use the cut block on all open field blocks.

It could be on a screen pass after the back catches the ball and the lineman is going downfield to block. He could use the cut block. It could be on a draw play when the linebacker starts to drop back. When the linebacker comes up, the guard used a cut block against him. We cut all open field blocks.

We had other plays when we cut blocked. We use the cut on quick pitches and similar plays. We would have the guard cut block on the quick pitch if he could get there in time.

Pass Blocking

The next thing I want to discuss is pass blocking. Some of the things I have seen here, I disagree with. I boxed. Ask me who the heavyweight champion at Penn State was in 1954? Dan Radakovich! I was the champion. I weighed 174 pounds. I beat Bull Smith who was a 235-pound noseguard. I kicked his ass.

Let me tell you what I learned as a boxer. I learned to get full extension with my arms. I learned to snap my wrist when I threw a jab. You snap the jab into the opponent. But one hand does not make a block. One hand is not going to block me or a defensive lineman. You can't do it with one hand. You must have two hands to be successful. You must have your hands on the defender.

The reason I have my arms fully extended is because I wanted to make contact first. I was tired of seeing offensive linemen always being in a recovery stage. Many of them had their arms in tight close to their body. That is the way many of them blocked. Some of them hit the defender with their head with a head butt. After they made contact, they ended up trying to recover as the defender came into them.

Boxing and pass blocking and run blocking in football are not the same. How do I really know that? One reason is because I boxed. Second, I ask you this question: who do you think was the first coach to use the drills with the hands and arms extended? I started those drills with the hands and arms extended.

After throwing a few punches in blocking Joe Greene, he wanted to know how I could block anyone by extending the arms and using my hands. I wanted to know how dumb I could be. You can't block anyone just with your arms and hands. If you only used one hand against the defender, they could take that one hand and knock it off to the side. Also, they can go to either side against the block.

But use of the hands is a lost art because I did this in 1974. We had the best pass protection in the league. The lost art in pass protection is being able to slide the hands against the defender. How many of you see the shoulder twist when you are in pass protection? Not one of you! You are 40 years behind times. If the defender turns his side or shoulder against the pass blocker, he should get both hands on the defender as he turns and knock him for a loop.

Guys that are teaching pass protection with the thumbs up have made James Harrison the defensive player of the year a couple of times. I know he ran an interception back for 100 yards in a Super Bowl. But all Harrison does is use the rip move. I see offensive coaches that teach their offensive linemen to lower one hand and to push against the defender that is using the rip move.

I watched film for 50 years, and I never saw a successful block against the rip move by pushing the defenders hip. That crap does not work. You do not stop the rip move with a block with one hand on the defender's hip. It doesn't work.

The other thing I learned was when I coached the defensive line in my early years. I taught the players to use their hands to stop all of the techniques the blockers used. The day after I put in our hand movements against the pass protectors, Joe Greene came to me and asked me what were we going to do if an offensive blocker used a rip technique against us? The offensive blocker would take his inside arm and rip up through the top arm of the defender. I told him that was a good question. I figured out what you do against that move.

All you do against the rip move is to move your hands together and place them on front of the blocker's chest. People talk about James Harrison. But really, he could not pass rush against me. I am an old man, and he could not get past me on his rip move. (Thanks to our two young coaches that assisted us on the blocking techniques.)

If you do not get anything from me from this clinic, you need to learn what we were doing 40 years ago. I know some of you were not even born at that time.

This is how it works. We line up a blocker and a defender. The offensive man places both hands on the defensive man's chest. The defender does a quick dip of the shoulder to one side or the other to represent the shoulder twist. The blocker slides his hands to the lower shoulder of the defender on the shoulder twist move.

The other thing I have to mention is this: if you bring your arms back and bend your elbows, you are going to get beat. Anything with the elbows back is a disaster. It was so bad, I got rid of the bench press in the weight room. We had the strongest players in the league. We went with an incline press with the arms up over the head. I wanted everything in the weight room like it was going to be similar to what we did on pass protection. We did not want the blockers to bend their elbows and shoot from the belly on their hand movements. The strength coach solved that problem for me.

Next, is the arm over move. The arm over move should be extinct because of the lockout of the hands. When I first started the arm over move, it was with Jon Kolb, who was our center. The defensive man used his near hand and grabbed his jersey at the top of the shoulder pad and pulled the blocker forward. The blocker had been taught to shuffle or to hop back with both feet to get the defender off his shoulder pad. As he hopped back, the defensive man brought him inside arm over the top of the blocker's near arm and did the swim techniques to get by the blocker.

We figured we had to do the opposite of what we had been doing if we wanted to be successful. So instead of hopping back, we pushed forward as the defender pulled the blocker. As we moved into the pass rusher, we stepped back with one foot to brace our push forward. We always bring the other arm and hand into the defender's chest area so we have more leverage against the defender. I really want to stress bringing the other hand into the chest area of the defender. One hand does not work on this move.

Next, we will show you the rip move. The defender grabs the blocker the same way with his outside hand on the top of the shoulder pad. He grabs cloth of the jersey. The defender pulls the blocker forward. As the defender starts hip rip move by dropping the shoulder, the blocker brings the other hand on the chest area of the defender. He gets both hands into the chest cavity of the defender.

Recovery Drills

I call these drills "recovery drills." The defender comes at the blocker with both hands and grabs at his head. We want to get both hands up in the chest area to break the momentum of the rusher.

Tony Wise came to visit me back in 1979, when I was with the Los Angeles Rams. Rich Saul and Dennis Harrah demonstrated these drills for us. They tried to break each other's neck. I had to stop them. I said, "Hey, let it go when you get a hand on the head."

We do the same drill with the defender grabbing the blocker's shoulder. Notice the hands do not go back. The hands come straight up into the defender's chest area.

From there, we move to the billy goat technique. The defender is going to try to hit the blocker in his stomach with his head. He is going to try to butt him like a billy goat with his head.

I forgot to mention this point. Where do you hit the defender that is rushing you? You hit him where he is the strongest. You hit him with the part of your body that is the strongest. Where is that? It is as high as it can be without hitting him in the head. The defender is strongest in the shoulders.

So you have to hit him in his shoulders. If he is turned sideways, you have to hit him on the outside of his shoulder at an angle. Basically, you have to hit the part of the shoulder that is sticking out. There is no such thing as hitting him in the middle of the chest or anything like that.

Hit the defender as high as you can, and fight strength with strength. If you want to know where your strength is as far as stance and position, go face a wall and put your hands up to the wall. Your strength is not by squatting down. Whereever the strongest position is for you where you can use the hands with the prongs you have, it is also the strongest position for you to move laterally. It just works out that way.

If you are squatting, you are not in the best hitting position. If you are standing straight up, you are not in the best hitting position. Somewhere in between, with the knees slightly bent, gives you more strength and you can move side to side.

As the defender comes at the blocker with his billy goat move, the blocker makes contact with both hands. He wants to give as little ground as possible. You do not just back up and continue to back up. You back up only enough to stay in front of the defender. That is it! You do not keep backing up and backing up. If you do that, the defender will run you off the playing field.

We do not just step back. We bounce back or hop back with both feet moving at the same time. You brace with the two prongs (arms and hands), and you brace with two feet on the ground. You will need to learn to stay parallel. You cannot move laterally with one foot in front of the other foot. You need to learn how to move laterally with the hands still in contact with the defender.

If the defender comes out of his stance low with his head down, the blocker must be able to get his hands on the shoulder pads of the defender very quickly. That is a common move by the defender.

Have any of you been to Louvre Museum in Paris, France? They have a statue of a good-looking woman there with no arms. Her name is Venus de Milo. Again, the statue has no arms.

The point I am making is this: we have a rush drill without arms. We call the drill "Venus." Hell, if you can't block Venus, you can't play for us. Some of your good players will not be able to block the defender on the Venus drill, at least in the beginning.

The defender comes at the blocker with his hands down to his waist. He does not try to use his hands. He spins after contact and tries to get past the blocker. We want the blocker to keep his hands extended, and we want his to stay in contact with the defender. He must slide his hands on the defender as he turns or spins on the rush.

The important thing about the Venus drill is to move your feet when you need to move them. We do not want the feet moving up and down as if you are running in place. It is important to move the feet when you need to move them. It is not pat, pat, pat, and pat. We want maximum resistance at all times. You must hit the rusher up high with the hands. If he hits the defender down low, he will get beat by the defender.

The other important point is to be able to lock out and be able to support your own body. If he has his hands close together with the elbows bent, he is nothing but an accordion player. You cannot be an accordion player. When you lock your arms out, you must be stiff enough where you can shuffle back to support your body. You keep that space between you and the defender. Coach Jim McNally called it "separation." It is important to maintain that separation between you and the defensive man.

There is one drill we did not do that I think is worth showing you. If you have a solid door that you can slam, you can teach your lineman how to do the lockout on the blocking techniques. We have the blocker face the door at a slight angle. We tell the blocker we are going to slam the door closed, and we are going to try to break his nose. The blocker has his hands on his knees. Then, we slam the door closed.

We want the blocker to lock his arms out when the door is slammed. He needs to extend the arms to stop the door from hitting him in the nose. I considered buying a door to take to the practice field, but I never did get the door for the practice field.

For those of you that want to teach a blocker to lock his elbows with his thumbs up, have him try to stop the slamming door with the thumbs up. You will see why I do not teach the blocker to have his thumbs up.

The important thing is to stop the defender's charge. It is important to be able to control the movable shield on the blocks. You must be able to stop the defender's rush and do the mirror drills as you move with the defender, keeping your hands in the chest area.

I do want to tell you about my book. The book is $29.95 plus tax which makes it $32.00 if you buy it today. If you want to order it from my website, the cost is $35.00. That is what it costs me to mail the book.

In the book, it will tell you how the Steel Curtain got started. Also, it will tell you how the locked out hands got started. The book contains a lot of stories. For example, how I beat the hell out of the mirror dodge drill, and the scarecrow drill. It tells the story of how I went to the wrong house in recruiting, and how I chased equipment men down looking for my gear.

I tell the story of how I walked into Rip Engle's bedroom at 4:00 a.m. His wife was in bed with her hair curlers on. The book has some good stories.

Tony Wise has one of my books. Dante Scarnecchia bought two of the books. He bought one for Bill Belichick, and one for himself. Harry has bought six of the books. He uses it for his library for his offensive line. If one of his linemen does good, they get to have a book for a couple of days. When the player brings the book back, they must be able to tell a story out of the book. That is what he uses the books for.

The first five chapters of the book are related to the Pittsburgh Steelers. They include information when I was the defensive line coach, and when I was the offensive line coach.

The next five chapters are about my time at Penn State. The stories include stories when I was with Rip Engle and later Joe Paterno. The last 10 chapters are on the 15 places that I coached.

Now that we have demonstrated the different drills, we are ready to show you the drills and moves on film. Thank you!

ABOUT THE AUTHOR

Dan Radakovich is a veteran offensive line coach with 48 years of coaching experience.

Radakovich is a former NFL football player and offensive line coach who helped coach the Pittsburgh Steelers to multiple Super Bowl wins in the 1970s. He spent 48 years in collegiate and professional coaching before his retirement in 2008.

Radakovich graduated from Penn State in 1957, and immediately began working on the coaching staff of the Nittany Lions, which he continued until 1969. He went to the University of Cincinnati in 1970, but joined the Pittsburgh Steelers in 1971.

Described as "lean, and blond, a center in his playing days," Radakovich was "a Western Pennsylvania guy who had been on Noll's staff in 1971 but resigned to take a coaching job in college football."

Radakovich subsequently returned to working with professional football, where he helped persuade Chuck Noll to draft Franco Harris out of Penn State.

After a stint with the University of Colorado, he coached the Steelers offensive line from 1974 to 1977. In 1978, Radakovich left Pittsburgh to work on the coaching staff of the San Francisco 49ers, and then he switched to the Los Angeles Rams in 1979.

He served on the Robert Morris University staff for several years after his retirement from the NFL.

THE WHAM, BLAST, BONG, AND PLAY-ACTION OFF OF WHAM

NFL Alumni

I want to thank you guys for being here this morning on the 8 o'clock shift. Some of the guys from last night were like sailors on leave and are not here, but that's all right. The guys that are here, I appreciate you being here.

When I was a young coach of 22 years, my first year of coaching, I went to a coaching clinic in Santa Monica, California. I went there because they were going to have one of the greatest coaches of all time speak on Saturday morning at 8 o'clock, a lot like this. Man, I was right there in the front row, and I had my papers out and I was ready to go. I was going to learn everything there was to learn about the game from this guy. At that time, he was one of the giants of college football.

He came walking in at 8 o'clock and got up on the stage and started talking. I thought, "Holy crap! This guy is really hung over." And he was *really* hung over. He could hardly talk, and his diagrams on the overhead made no sense whatsoever. I thought to myself, "I am not ever going to do that."

I want to make it beneficial to you guys sitting out here who have paid good money to be here, and want to come away with something. This is important to me, it really is. Having said that, I am going to tell you how we run certain plays within the offense. I am not going to tell you all of the calls. If I gave you all the calls, I would have to lock all the doors and keep you here for life, because that is how Coach Belichick would want it. I will tell you that the center is going to make a call or the tackle is going to make a call, and then you guys can figure that stuff out. If you have any questions, shout them out because I want to get all of your questions answered before I leave today.

I had a young coach send me a letter a couple of weeks ago. He said a lot of really nice things, but he was also looking for some advice as to what he could do to make himself a better coach. I immediately though of something that Mark Twain once said. He said that if God wanted you to talk more than listen, he would have given you two mouths and one ear. I think the most important thing that you can do as a young coach is to listen.

One of the greatest guys I have ever worked for was Raymond Berry. He was the quintessential listener. When you talked, he looked straight at you, and he wrote down anything that you said that he thought was important. That would be my advice to any young coach that is sitting out there today. Listen to everything that is being said. Like last night, you heard three really, really great offensive line coaches. They all talked about basically the same thing: the outside zone play. None of them said it the same way. They all said it in their own way, but they arrived at the same point. For us, that is really the essence of coaching. There is really no wrong way or right way to run the outside zone. But there is "our way" of running the outside zone play. You saw three examples of that last night. I think that is hugely important.

Another thing those three guys were good at last night was painting mental images in the minds of their players. If the players listen to what you have to say and they can see it in their minds, because you have painted a great picture, they have a great chance to do what you want them to do. That is what coaching is all about. I really enjoyed listening to those guys last night. That is what these clinics are all about.

We are going to talk about the wham play today. We are not going to talk about the outside zone. We are going to talk about the wham or what some people call the blast play. We have another name for the play, called the bong play. There are no drug references there. I will try to leave some time for questions and answers, if I can.

I have a list up here on the overhead. I know it is not on PowerPoint®. I am a lot like Coach Trickett; I do not know how to do it. I ain't doin it, either!

WHAM PLAYS

Plays That Are Complementary Runs That "Protect" Core Runs, Formations, and Motions That You Want to Use

These are not plays you are going to run 12 times a game. You may run it four times in one week, and the next week you may not run it at all. We were looking to run about 35 to 45 wham plays in a given season. I know there are a lot of you who run a wide open spread offense and are thinking, I don't know about this wham stuff. There are some of you who do not have any tight ends in your offense. For you guys, this might not do you a lot of good. If you do have at least one tight end on the field, you can still do things with this concept.

Plays That Are Used to Cut the Defense in Half

"Cut the defense in half" is the phrase we use. We are going to wham a defensive lineman, and outside of that we are going to zone block. On the backside, we are going to either gap or man block the backside. We are cutting the defense in half and going to try to isolate one half of the defense. We hope we are not going to run this against a team that has a two-gap system, where they have both hands on your blocker and move down the line with you.

Plays That Are Not Finesse Plays. They Are Plays That Allow Us to Play in a Physical Mannor

A lot of people think because we were the Patriots, we were a finesse-only team. We did like to take pride in the physicality of how we played the game. We ran the ball as well as any team. We like to run the ball. We like balance in the offense. If we are playing the way we want to play we are going to be at 50/50 run to pass.

Plays That Give the Defense More Things to Defend Especially Play-Action Passes Off of Wham Actions

We want to give the defense more things to think about, even though we may not plan on running the play in the upcoming game. We probably will have the blast or wham play-action included in almost every game. We do it because it is a great play-action play. The wham play and the play-actions off of them really gives the defense a lot to think about and that is what we are after.

IMPORTANT

These Plays Have a Short "Shelf Life"

If you run a play eight times a game, plays five through eight are not going to be as effective as the first few times you ran the play. Because of this, you really want to intermittently run it. You want to choose your spots and mix them in.

You Can Not Give the Defense the Same Looks. You Must Change The Formations and Motions.

You cannot run the same plays every week. You have to be a little more creative than that. You want to be able to do a lot of different things off of the same formations or motions.

Avoid Running Them at the Same Defender. Watch for Substitutions!

If we run the wham at a really good defender and have success with it, we are not going to run it at that same defender again. Even though they are not rocket scientists over there on the other side of the ball, they are not idiots either. They are going to get better at playing it the more times they see it. You run it at a guy, and if you have success with it, you wait for his substitute to come out there. This is the approach we have taken with this play over the years. We choose our spots because we want to get the very most that we can out of the play.

In 1999, when Bill came up from the Jets we all got together with Charlie Weis, who came as the offensive coordinator. Charlie put in an offensive system that was a combination of the Ron Erhardt system he brought from college to the Patriots, and stuff from Dan Henning from the Washington system when they were together with the Jets. One of the plays from that system was the Wham play.

The first play I want to show you is the flash play (Diagram #1). You line up a fullback or a second tight end and he motions in and seals the backside edge. You run right 34, inside zone. This was a core play in our offense when we all got together in 1999. What protected this play was the wham.

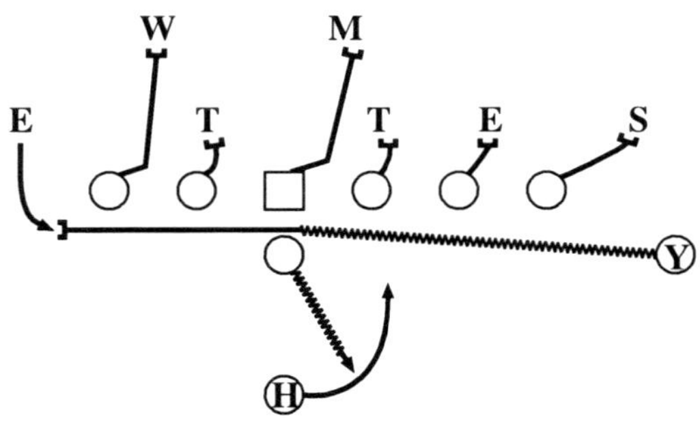

Diagram #1. Flash Play

What Is Wham?

The fullback or tight end will wham block the first defensive lineman from the frontside A gap to the backside. We will apply inside zone rules and techniques outside of the wham block and gap or man blocking on the backside.

This is what the play looks like against an even spaced defense (Diagram #2). We are whamming the first lineman from the frontside A gap to the backside. We take the F-back in short motion and bring him in where he goes all the way back and whams the backside tackle. Outside of that block, we are running inside zone or what we call "ride 34." The wham is using 4- or 5-hole zone blocking.

We have a frontside slip with the center and onside guard. The onside tackle and tight end angle block their guys out. Because this is man, the backside guard jab steps and then goes behind the tackle to the defensive end and seals the backside edge. We put the tackle through for the Will linebacker. We have cut the defense in half at the backside tackle and isolated everybody to the frontside

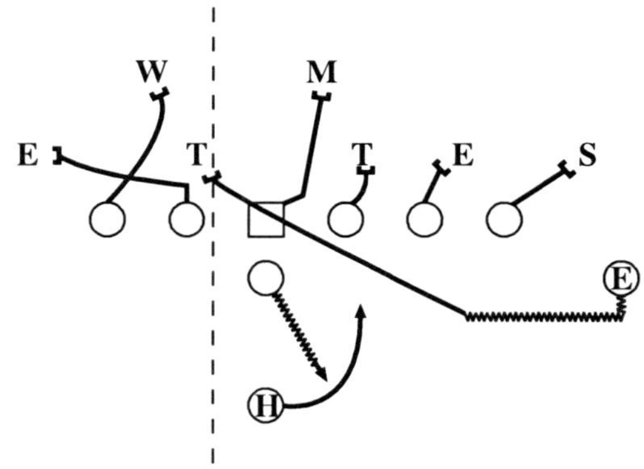

Diagram #2. Wham vs. Even

of the play. It makes the back's job a little easier to see where we are trying to go when he doesn't have to read the whole front.

To see how it looks against 3-4 spacing, we are whamming the zero technique nose tackle (Diagram #3). What we do to facilitate that is we have the center to declare himself out. He essentially snaps the ball and pulls flat to seal the backside edge. On the frontside, we are blocking ride 34, or inside zone. The playside guard and tackle are blocking their inside zone techniques. We are essentially using zone blocks to the backside as well.

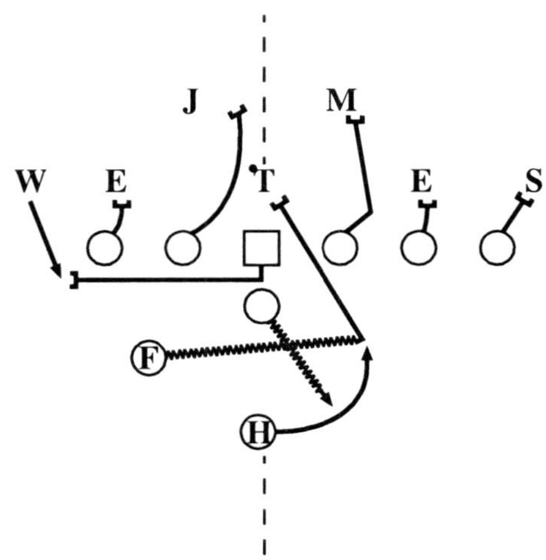

Diagram #3. Wham vs. 3-4

In this look, we tell the backside guard to take his cutoff angle off of the backside hip of the noseguard, going as fast as he can go. If the noseguard angles back to him, he takes him. The wham blocker then climbs to the second level and takes the Jack linebacker. If the noseguard plays toward the wham block, which they frequently do, the backside guard has to do a really good job of cutting off the Jack linebacker.

If we came up against under spacing, we would be whamming the offset noseguard (Diagram #4).

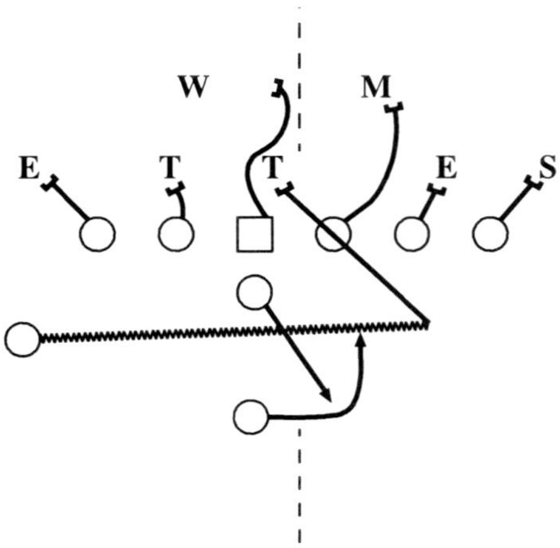

Diagram #4. Wham vs. Under

The center would be making a gap call to the backside. The center, backside guard, and tackle would essentially have the defensive tackle, the end, and the Will linebacker. The center has to slip to the inside of the noseguard and then stack behind him to get the Will linebacker, especially if he fast reads and tries to get over the top. This play rarely gets cut back behind the noseguard. To the frontside, it is just inside zone.

Slip and stack by the center, what does that look like? It can be a club, swim, stack to get behind the noseguard, and wall off the backside linebacker. It literally looks like that.

That is the wham against even, over, under, or odd defenses. Let me discuss formations and motions. You can run this with a fullback in a far alignment, motioning over to a near alignment and whamming the first down lineman (Diagram #5).

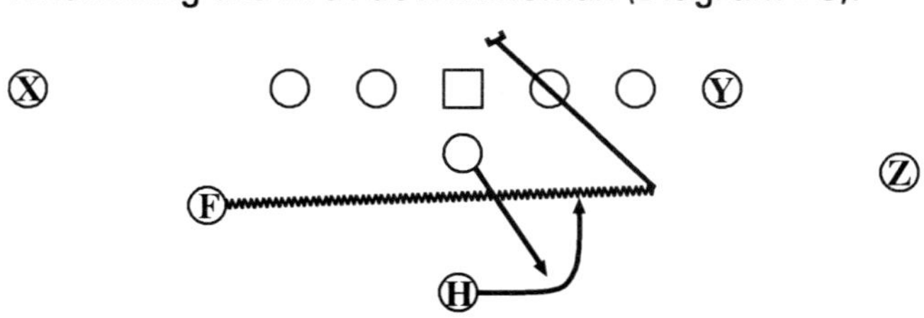

Diagram #5. Motion: Far to Near

You can put both tight ends on the line of scrimmage and say we are going to make this a wham block to the guard bubble side of the defense. It would then become a check with me play. It could be the Y stemming off and going across and whamming, or the F stemming off and going across and whamming (Diagram #6). It could be either one.

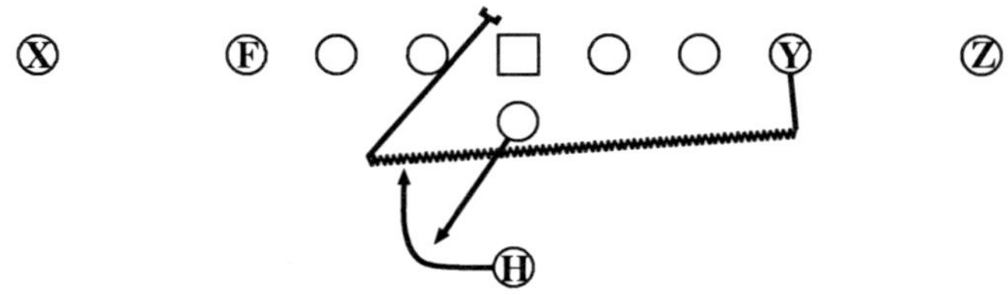

Diagram #6. Motion: 2x2

I really like running it from a bunch formation (Diagram #7). You will find you have a lot more space because the defense likes to put the Sam outside the point guy in a bunch. They do not want the Sam to be outleveraged. We get more space when that happens, which is really important to us.

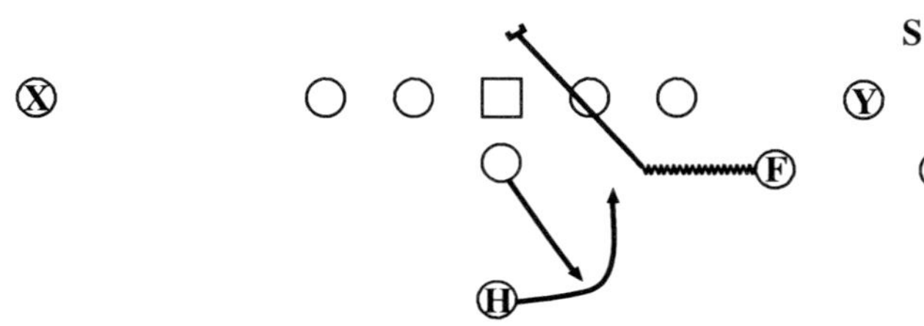

Diagram #7. Motion: Bunch

We would short motion the F-back and he would go ahead and wham the defender. Now, I need to make this point to you. Because you are using motion, you really need to position the Z-back into proximity where he can block the first force. What we do is put him in an open split so he is right there and he can go get the strong safety. You might have to protect that by running passes off of it. This is really important to the success of the play.

In Diagram #6, we might bring the X and the Z in a tighter proximity to the two tight ends so they could go in and block for us, not knowing which side we are going to run it to until it was mandated by the quarterback at the line of scrimmage.

You could run it from an extended 2x2 formation (Diagram #8) or from an extended 3x1 formation (Diagram #9).

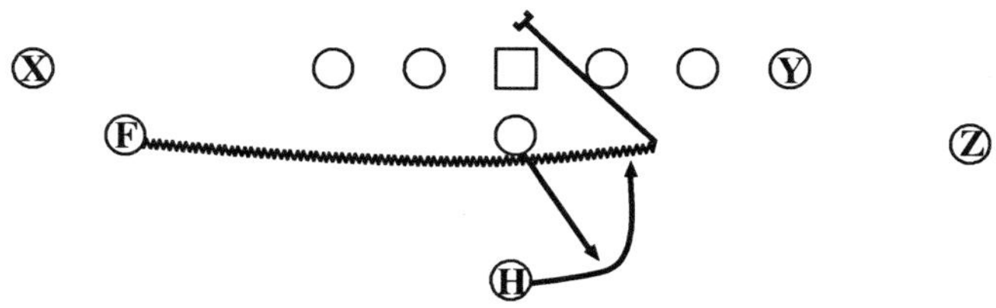

Diagram #8. Extended 2x2 Formation

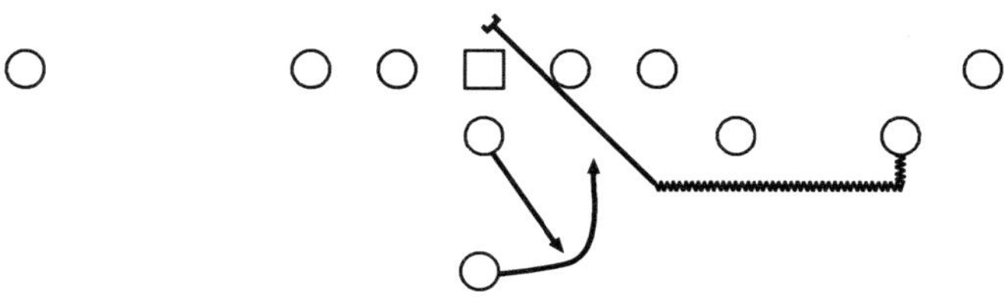

Diagram #9. Extended 3x1 Formation

Really, it can be run from whatever your mind can put together. The most important thing about what we have been talking about is to get the man in motion, in an alignment position to facilitate the wham block.

The other thing is to get the force block either by X or Z, depending on which way you run with it, in order to take care of force. We do not give this guy a call, he sees the front. You can do the math. If you see a three technique to your side, you can figure that there is a bubble on the guard to the other side so you are whamming the tackle.

I have to be honest with you, which is why I am here, to tell you honestly. If you motion the guy, sometimes the front stems. If that happens, you have to block it on the run. If you are solid in your rules and how you are teaching it, I think you really have a great chance to get it done anyway. This play handles a lot of movement and stunts because you are zoned, or you are gapped on a lot of these fronts so it makes it that much easier.

We will also run from three open, a one-back variation of wham. I really want you to remember this because this is really where we have arrived with the wham play (Diagram #10).

We do with the Y the same thing we just talked about doing with the F or the fullback. We run short motion and wham the first down lineman from the frontside A gap to the backside. This gives a play from 3 open that we can run at a six-man front.

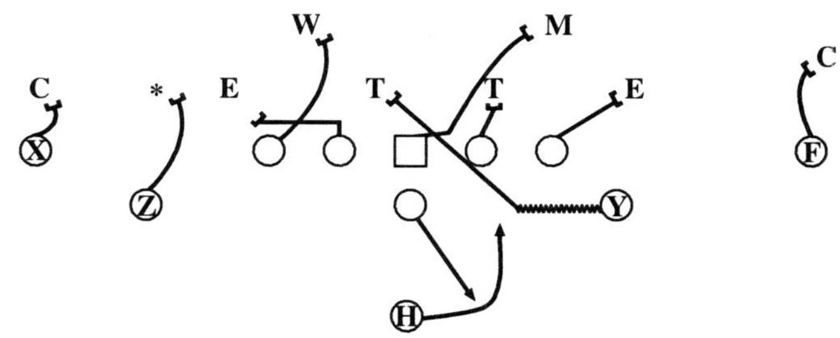

* = BE READY FOR DEFENSIVE MOVEMENT

Diagram #10. 3 Open

We have to call the Mike on the frontside, and you guys have watched us, Tom Brady points out the Mike on everything. He calls it on runs and passes. We want everyone in the formation, unilaterally, to see who the Mike linebacker is. That is important to us, and that is why he is the guy that does it. All of our quarterbacks have to be able to do that.

We can run it by motioning the Y all the way across and whamming the frontside noseguard (Diagram #11).

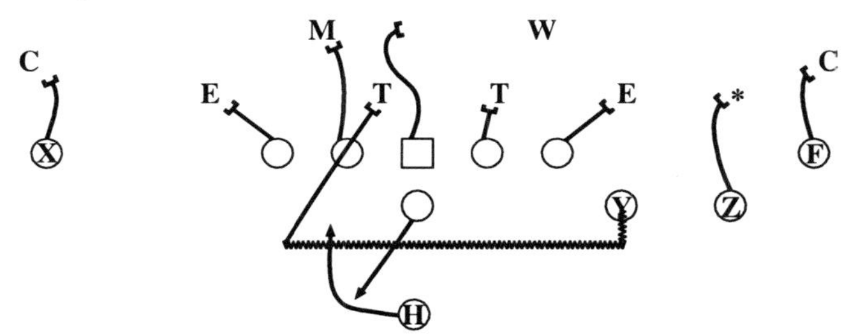

Diagram #11. Frontside A Gap

I said to be ready for defensive movement because one of two things happen when you are in a one-back formation and you motion the Y. Especially if you move him across the ball. If the linebackers are playing man coverage, they will switch. In that case, we switch them on the run. Sometimes, the front will adjust over and you have to adjust to it on the run. That is part of running these plays.

Following is an example of where we have to put through the backside guard in front of the guy we are wham blocking (Diagram #12).

If the defender spikes or carries the frontside guard, he tire arms him. The wham blocker has to be able to adjust, once again, to the second level. He would block the Will linebacker if that happened.

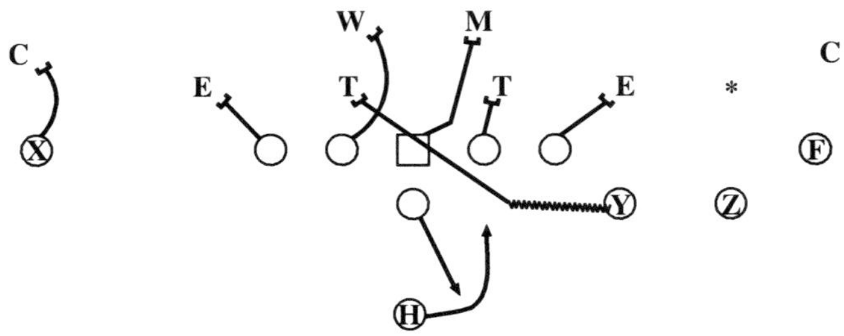

Diagram #12. Through Block

Now let's talk about the blast play. About 10 years ago, we were sitting in an offensive meeting, and Coach Belichick comes in and says, "I want to wham the defensive tackle to the frontside." Then he walked out.

This is my feeling on that. When the head coach comes in and he has been doing some looking and he has been doing some thinking, and he comes in with a suggestion, you owe him one of two things. One, you figure out how to make it happen. Two, you owe him a response that placates him and lets him know why you think it is a bad idea. You owe him that. If you do not have a good reason why not, you better be ready to carry it all the way through.

In this case, he did not think it through, other than we were seeing a lot of teams playing overs, but what happened if they were playing under? Then what are you going to do. The other thing is we aren't going to call it wham because wham is the first down lineman to the playside A gap to the backside. We are going to call it blast.

What Is Blast?

The fullback or tight end will blast the first defensive lineman from the frontside B gap to the backside. When we first put this in, the onside guard always had the Mike linebacker. Possible zone with the onside tackle. This now becomes 6 or 7 hole zone blocking outside of the blast block. The backside is still zone or man blocking. Formations and motions are essentially the same as the wham. Once again, the Z has the force.

The play is zone blocked a little wider because of the proximity of the guy you are blasting (Diagram #13).

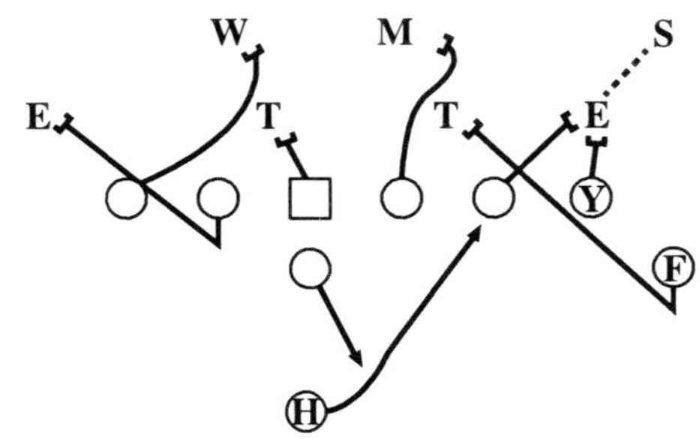

Diagram #13. Blast

As I said, we were seeing a lot of over fronts. We have a frontside combo block with the frontside tackle and tight end. That is a hard double-team block on the end in the 6 hole until the Sam declares to the tight end or inside to the tackle. We are blasting the defensive tackle. What do you think the guard is going to do? He is going to slip and stack. He clubs, he swims, he stacks, and he cuts of the Mike linebacker, just as the center did previously. The backside can be man or gap blocking. In this case, it is man blocking. We are putting the tackle through, and the guard will come out to the defensive end.

If the frontside defensive tackle spikes in front of the guard's face, the guard will keep him and the blast blocker will climb to the second level and block the Mike.

So we satisfied Bill. But what happens if they play an under? We are still going to blast the frontside tackle, but now he is the nose tackle (Diagram #14).

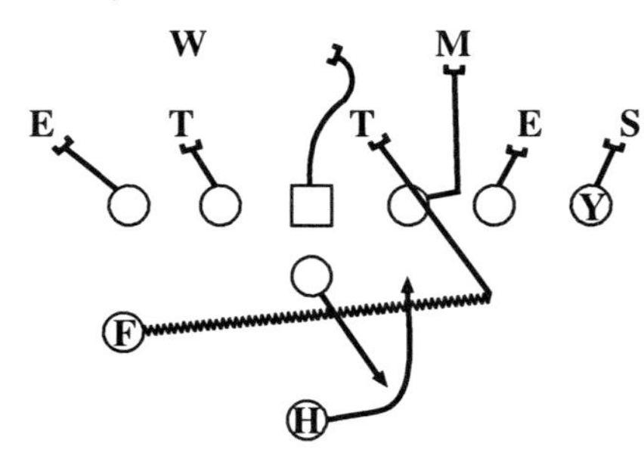

Diagram #14. Blast vs. Under

What does that play look like? It looks like wham. Inadvertently, blast became wham. We ended up with the best of both worlds. We were going to blast the 3 technique or we were going to blast the nose tackle, and we didn't have to call two plays. We can just call blast, and essentially they do one in the same. That was a huge thing for us because it scratched one play off of the run sheet.

How did we put all of this together? Blast is blast, partially wham when we are in two backs or two tight ends. Wham became three open, one back for us, just like I showed you. That is the truth. That is how we arrived at this.

You can see that, if you were an offensive lineman or a blast blocker, how much fun this would be (Diagram #15). The frontside guard pulls and traps the backside defensive tackle. The blast blocker comes in motion and then blocks back on the frontside defensive tackle. The center would punch himself through and get the Mike linebacker. We have a 6-hole zone combo block to the frontside with the tackle and tight end. The backside guard hand checks the defensive tackle and then comes out to get the backside defensive end. About two years ago, we decided to run it this way with either an over or even look.

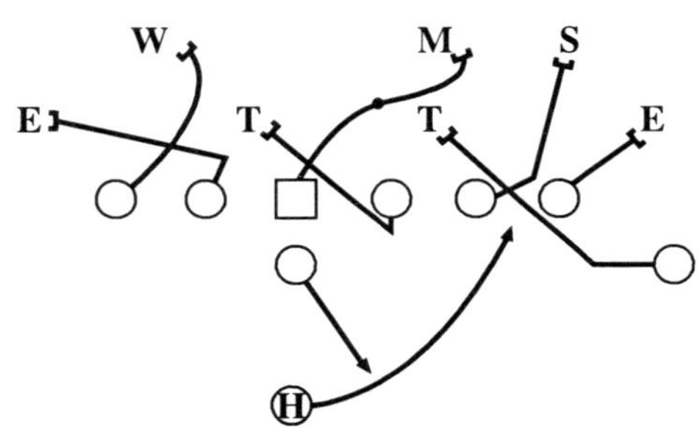

Diagram #15. Blast Final

The reactions that you get from the defense when all of that happens are really amazing. I am talking about some really great football players. In particular the Mike linebacker, because what he sees is the guards going one way and the backs going another way. All of a sudden, the center has him and he is a dead man. He really has no chance. There is just too much going on for him. The frontside guard has it easy by going back and trapping the defensive nose tackle.

Question: What is the wham or blast blocker looking for when he comes in motion?

We are assuming the defender he is blocking is not moving. We are going to make that assumption. As he comes in motion, his shoulders are perpendicular to the line of scrimmage, and there is a point where he has to start to throttle down. When he gets to the right spot, it becomes an angled drive block for him. Can he be too far away? Absolutely. Can he be too close? Yes, and when the defense sees him shuffling his feet, they probably have a pretty good idea it is a wham block. There is a happy place there in the middle. It is an angled drive block, assuming there is no upfield movement.

Question: If you have to A gap down linemen, how do you handle that?

The center will choke back on the one guy. We are still whamming the frontside A gap. We would have to put the tackle through and bring the guard out on the backside.

Question: If the wham is at the 4 and 5 hole, and the blast is at the 6 and 7 hole, what is the difference with the angle of the back?

The back has to see what everyone else sees. If he sees we are blasting a 3 technique, he starts essentially as inside zone, but then widens after he gets the ball. It happens a lot faster than I just said. He is not going downhill and then coming out. It is a subtle drop step, then a crossover, and then he starts to widen. The quarterback knows he has to widen to get him the ball at a little bit wider handoff point. Why? Because if the 3 technique gets up the field and we hit him sideways, he is kind of in the backfield.

What Is Bong?

Bong is the three open, one-back version of blast. We had wham where we were whamming the first down lineman from the frontside A gap to the backside. We had blast where we were blasting the first down lineman from the B gap to the backside. With the blast, we have two tight ends or two backs, which some people call 12 personnel. We wanted to run blast from a one-back set. We didn't want to call it blast because it has its own rules. We came up with bong. That is what coaches do; they make stuff up. Bong is essentially the same as blast (Diagram #16).

We are hitting the 6 or 7 hole. If we were running against an under front, it would be just like 34 wham.

Let's go over play-action protections with this. I am telling you right now, fellas, anytime we call it, sign me up. It is the best. It is the absolute best because you are man or zone on one side, and essentially slide protecting the backside. It is an

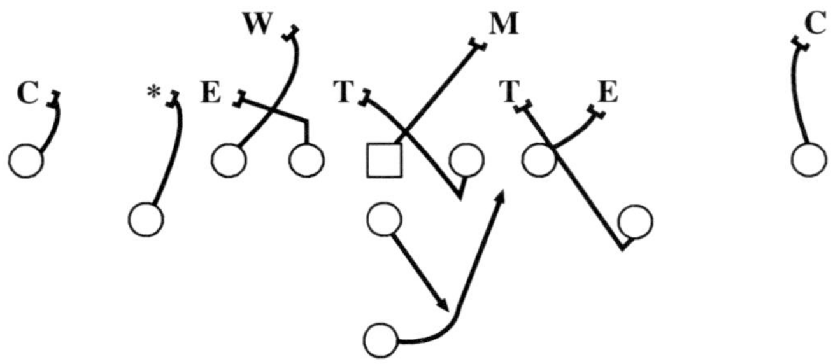

Diagram #16. Bong

eight-man protection system. The tight end is in, and the back has the strong safety. You are showing the defense the hardest of play-action that there is. You are throwing the ball into intermediate zones. You are running slants, skinny posts, end cuts, and occasionally we have thrown crossing routes with it. The reactions of the linebackers are exactly what you want. When they see the play-action, they are fast reading and hitting it up inside. This is just a really great play-action. There are no excuses for anyone to play at anything other than at the highest aggressive level. We all say, "Sell the run." Sometimes you can't really sell the run when you have slide protection up front. This is how we block it (Diagram #17).

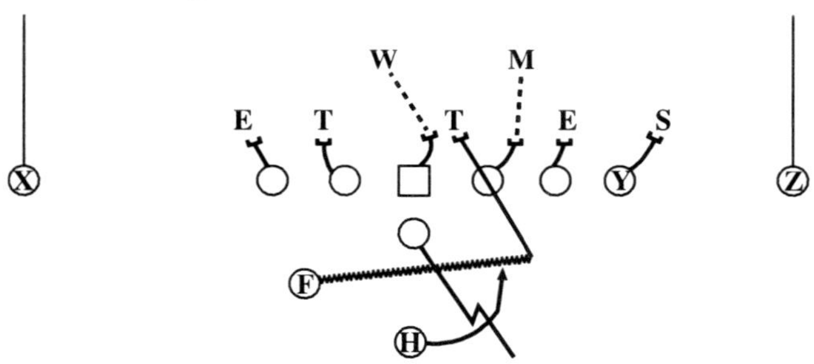

Diagram #17. Play-Action vs. Under

We block it pretty much like the run, except we do not put the center on the Mike linebacker. The frontside is the zone side of it, so they will make a call that says the guard and tackle have the Mike and defensive end. The blast blocker along with the center has the noseguard and Will linebacker. The backside guys have the two men in front of them.

If we are going against an over front, the F and the onside guard have the tackle and Mike, just like they would on the run play. They are combo blocking the tackle and Mike. (Diagram #18)

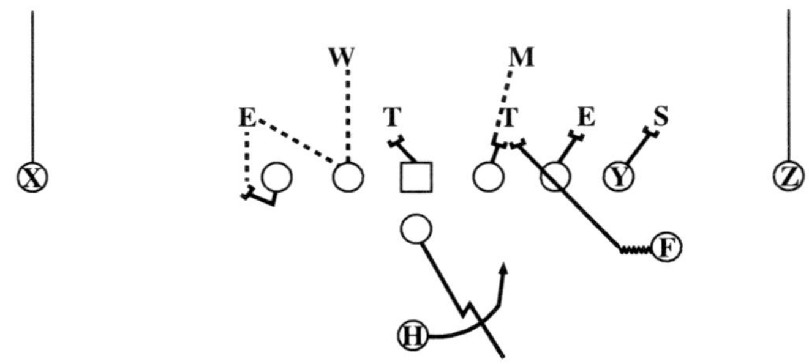

Diagram #18. Play-Action vs. Over

The three offensive linemen to the backside have the three box defenders to their side. I have drawn up a couple of more looks because you might want to know. Following is the play against a 3-4 look (Diagram #19).

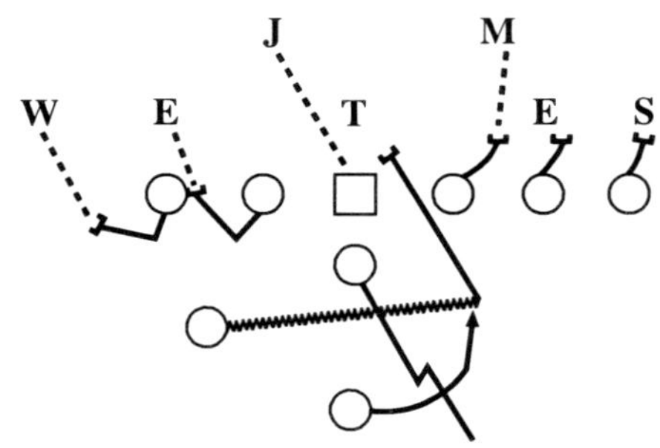

Diagram #19. Play-Action vs. 3-4

As you remember, we are blasting the first down lineman from the frontside B gap to the backside. We are blasting the noseguard. It is really a combo for the blast blocker and the center versus the noseguard and the Jack linebacker. The two linemen to the backside have the two defensive linemen to their outside.

Against an even defense, it is much like what we just talked about earlier. The Will is on the line of scrimmage and blocked by the tackle (Diagram #20).

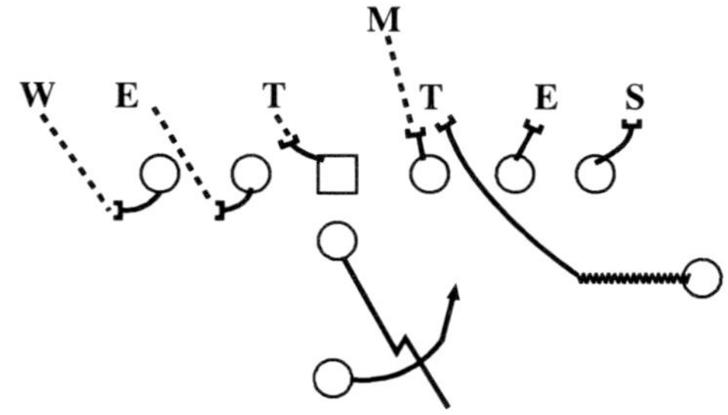

Diagram #20. Play-Action vs. Even

This is what it looks like against what we call a diamond defense. You may call it bear (Diagram #21).

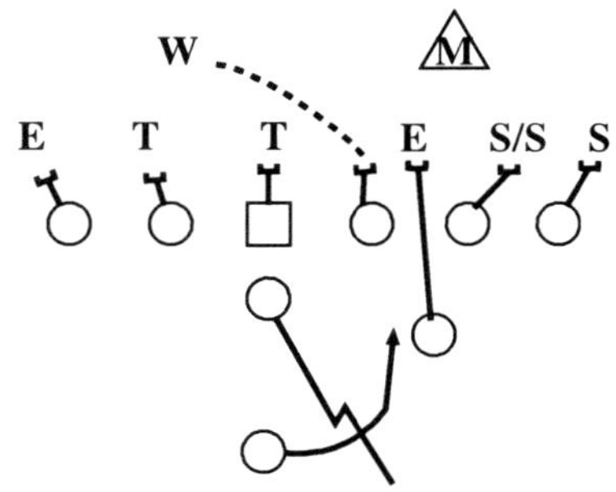

Diagram #21. Play-Action vs. Diamond (Bear)

The right guard has to look all the way to the Will linebacker because you have an eight-man box. The halfback is in the protection and he along with the right tackle trade out against the strong safety/Jack linebacker and the Mike linebacker.

If we lined up and saw a bear, we would really only run it against a seven-man bear defense. You really can't run it against eight because the Z has force, and he either has to motion and block the Sam on the line or motion inside and block the strong safety. We know that is not going to go very well for us. If it is a seven-man bear and the safety was high enough, you could still do it. You would blast the 3 technique. The guard now goes through and the tackle now has the Mike and the tight end has the Sam.

Fellas, there really isn't a better play-action pass protection you could want that is better than this one. I really believe that.

If you have all of these components in place with the blast concepts along with the play-actions with it, you really have a lot of good stuff going for you.

My time is up. I appreciate you being here with me so early in the morning. Thank you.

ABOUT THE AUTHOR

Dante Scarnecchia is a 41-year coaching veteran, who enjoyed 29 seasons as an NFL assistant. He has the longest coaching tenure in Patriots' history, coaching 27 seasons on the Patriots sidelines.

Scarnecchia has the distinction of being the only coach in franchise history to be a member of all six of its Super Bowl teams. He has been on the Patriots coaching staff during 13 of the franchise's 16 playoff appearances and has coached in 30 of the 34 playoff games in team history.

In the 2011 season, the offensive line helped produce the best rushing season in more than 20 years for the Patriots. New England averaged 4.4 yards per carry and totaled 2,278 yards and 21 rushing touchdowns. The offensive line also helped to consistently sustain drives, as the Patriots led the league in drives of 10 plays or longer (38) and in rushing first downs (145).

In 2007, Scarnecchia was named SI.com's NFL Assistant Coach of the Year. Anchored by an offensive line that sent three players to the Pro Bowl (center Dan Koppen, tackle Matt Light, and guard Logan Mankins), the Patriots offense broke several NFL records, including points scored and touchdowns scored. The offensive line powered a Patriots rushing attack that posted the franchise's highest average yards per rush in 22 years (4.10). The offensive line also allowed just 21 sacks in the regular season, the lowest total for the franchise since the NFL adopted a 16-game schedule. Protected by the line, NFL MVP Tom Brady broke the NFL record for touchdown passes in a season (50) and led the league in both passing yards (4,806, also a franchise record) and passer rating (117.2, also a franchise record).

New England's protection up front was a significant contributor to the team's three Super Bowl winning seasons. In 2004, the line opened holes for running back Corey Dillon to set a single-season franchise record with 1,635 rushing yards and led the NFL with 109.0 yards per game. In 2003, the offensive line did not allow a sack in any of the team's three post-season games despite 126 pass attempts. In 2001, Scarnecchia worked with a unit that featured three new starters, but still produced a powerful rushing attack and a balanced passing attack on the way to the franchise's first Super Bowl victory.

Prior to becoming offensive line coach, Scarnecchia coached the Patriots special teams units for two seasons (1997–1998).

Scarnecchia originally joined the Patriots and made his NFL coaching debut in 1982 as a member of Ron Meyer's staff. He coached the tight ends and special teams for the Patriots for seven seasons (1982–1988) before moving on to Indianapolis with Meyer in 1989. He rejoined the Patriots in 1991 after spending two seasons (1989–1990) as the Colts' offensive line coach. From 1991 to 1992, he coached the tight ends and special teams on Dick MacPherson's staff. On November 4, 1992, MacPherson fell ill and appointed Scarnecchia to serve as the team's spokesman in his absence. Scarnecchia fulfilled the obligation for seven of the Patriots' final eight games and held the responsibilities of the head coach for both of the Patriots' victories that season.

In 1993, he was the only Patriots assistant retained from the previous staff. He was appointed special assistant from 1993 to 1994, which was redefined as defensive assistant from 1995 to 1996. During that time, he assisted defensive coordinator Al Groh with the development of the team's linebacking corps.

His coaching career began in 1970 as the offensive line coach at California Western University. He moved to Iowa State University in 1973, where he served as the assistant offensive line and assistant defensive backfield coach. He spent the 1975 and 1976 campaigns at Southern Methodist University, before becoming the University of the Pacific's offensive line coach and recruiting coordinator from 1977 through 1978. In 1979, Scarnecchia coached at Northern Arizona University and then accepted an opportunity to return to Meyer's staff at SMU as the offensive line coach in 1980 and 1981. In 1982, Meyer was hired as the head coach of the New England Patriots, and Scarnecchia was among a number of the SMU assistants who joined Meyer's staff in New England.

Mark Staten

THE INS AND OUTS OF MICHIGAN STATE'S OUTSIDE ZONE PLAY

Michigan State University

The greatest thing about this clinic, if you haven't been here before, is you are going to get answers to your questions. You are not going to get the normal generic "This is our program; thank you very much." I am going to give you some ideas about what we try to do in our system with the outside zone game.

When you look at our offensive line team picture, you will see I am the biggest guy in the picture with the exception of one walk-on. Our starting right tackle was 6'3 1/2" Our starting guard was 6'5", and he got hurt going into the bowl game, so we started a guy who was 6'3". Our starting center was 6'1" on a good day. Our other guard was 6'2", and our left tackle was a 6'5 1/2" freshman. This required us to do a lot with the hands. We studied what the defenders were trying to do, so we worked on taking away the hands of the defenders. I will talk about those techniques as we go.

I want to show you our value statements for our 2013 team. Coach Dantonio has each new team come up with their statements, and it becomes what we are all about (Table #1).

When you look at the list you see things like *hard work, accountability*, and *toughness*. If you saw the Big 10 championship game or the Rose Bowl game you saw two teams really getting after it at a very high level. You also see the word *opportunity*. We are all blessed to be here today because someone gave you the opportunity at some point in time to be involved in this phenomenal game. What you do with that opportunity is up to you.

I was talking to Bob Wylie earlier, and he made the comment that sometimes people are afraid to fail. I told Bob when he called to invite me here that I come to the C.O.O.L. Clinic to learn from guys like Paul Alexander, Jim McNally, Bob Wylie, and Dante Scarnecchia. Bob said, "Hey it's your turn. This is your opportunity." I found out later that he takes the young line coaches and he feeds them to the wolves first, so I thank you for that, Bob.

Let me move to our run blocking fundamentals. Any great coach is a great thief, and I stole these from someone. We have these posted in the back of our room. When our offensive linemen come in, they see this every day.

RUN BLOCKING FUNDAMENTALS: FOUR CRITICAL ELEMENTS IN RUN BLOCKING

- *Eyes on Aiming Point:* Speed to the target is essential.
- *Establish Leverage:* Get your pads under the defense.
- *Elbows In:* If they are in tight, your hands will be in the right place. Keep hands low—not on the top part of the defender's pads.
- *Drive Your Backside Knee:* Knees must come under your armpit. Drive the backside knee and follow with the play side foot.

Eyes on the Aiming Point

Speed is essential. How many of you stand behind your players in almost every drill they run, and coach them from there? The majority of you do, because that is the way we were taught to do it. A few years ago, someone told me to stand in front and watch them. It doesn't have to be all of the time. Do it in certain drills so you can see where their eyes are. See what they are looking at. You will be shocked, even at our level, how many guys

2013 Michigan State Football
What We Value

1. *Hard Work*

   It takes no ability and there is no *substitute*.

2. *Accountability*

   The green jersey is a physical representation of a standard of excellence. By wearing it, we agree to hold ourselves and our teammates to this standard. For this reason, the *jersey is always earned*, never given.

3. *Toughness*

   - Physical: We have trained our bodies to excel in any situation they are put into. Discomfort, pain, and fatigue will not be deterrents, but rather will be embraced and overcome.
   - Mental: *We will not be broken.* Our concentration, focus, and goals are not affected by momentary hardships and setbacks.

4. *Preparation*

   Proper preparation during the week allows us to play with the speed, focus, and tenacity that will be demanded of us at game time. We will *anticipate the difficult by managing the easy.*

5. *Execution*

   Execution starts and ends with these two things: knowing your job and doing your job. Teams that win championships consist of players who do their job from the first snap to the last. *We must find the inches.*

6. *Opportunity*

   Michigan State Football has given us a platform to succeed in areas well beyond the playing field. We have the opportunity to *earn an education* that prepares us for life after football. We have the opportunity to *make a difference* in our community in a way that has meaningful and lasting impact. We have the opportunity to *represent* our university in all aspects of our lives.

Win Today! Win Forever! Chase It!

Table #1. 2013 Value Statements

close their eyes at the moment of impact. That is why you will see me on the tape in front, coaching my guys. Make sure you see where their eyes are going and that they are going to their aiming point.

Establish Leverage

That is a no-brainer. Get your pads under the defense.

Elbows In

We are constantly talking about keeping the elbows in. We are constantly talking about keeping the thumbs up. We talk about keeping their weight on their instep.

Drive Your Backside Knee

What that means is you have got to get your second step down. One way or the other, you have got to get that second step down. Some guys might need to lose a little ground on the first step in order to gain ground on the second step.

As you watch your guys, each guy is a little different. We are all offensive linemen, so we are a little different anyway. As you coach your guy, make sure you are coaching that guy. Make sure you are using what that guy does best in order to help your program. We would all like to do it the same way, me included. When you are dealing with guys from 6'1" to 6'6", there are a lot of differences between each guy. Some guys have long arms; some guys have short arms, and so forth.

OUTSIDE ZONE PLAY

- Stay simple
- Main principle covered/uncovered rules upfront
- Tailback reads EMLOS
- Make it fit your system
    - ✓ Two-back, one-back, tight end side, split side

Let's talk about the outside zone play. It is our stretch run play. It is our 36-37 run play.

We try to stay simple. We do the outside zone in two different ways. We will go with covered and uncovered, and then we go with pin and pull. I will talk about that as we go. We will pin the 3 technique and pull the guard. You would be amazed to see some of the combinations that we end up blocking with it. I think the first time we ran it, we actually stumbled across it. From that point on, we thought, "Hey this works. Let's go ahead and coach it."

We will talk about the main principles of covered and uncovered first. The covered and uncovered rules are very simple. If I am covered with a 5 technique and I am the right tackle running an openside outside zone, and the guy inside of me is uncovered, he is going to short pull and he is going to help me. So if I get the 5 technique spiking inside, he is going to help me pick that up, and I will work up to the linebacker. Our footwork is the same as if you were covered to the frontside. If I am a covered tight end, it is the same. If I am a covered guard or tackle, it is the same.

Where problems start to happen is when you get 2is, when you have inside shades on the guards. Now he has to help the center, and the tackle is all by himself. What happens to the tackle now? He doesn't stretch it as much because he is worried about the 5-technique spike. We have found ways to pin with the guard and pull the center, and the double-team will be with the center and right tackle. We will talk more about this in a minute. It is just another way to get it done, and it works for us.

Make it fit your system. Whatever offense you run, you can make the outside zone fit your system. I think this will help you be a better football team. A year ago (in 2012), we averaged 30 yards less per game than what we did this year, and we had Le'Veon Bell, who is now playing with the Pittsburgh Steelers. I think this play helped our average go up a whole yard every time we called it.

Let's take a look at it.

STRETCH RULES

- Wide zone blocking scheme
- Offensive line 18-inch splits: normal alignment
- Back read EMLOS
- Zone reach or tight reach
    - ✓ Covered with help: zone reach
    - ✓ Covered without help: tight reach
- Footwork
    - ✓ Lateral lead to position
    - ✓ Through the crotch of the defender
    - ✓ Up the field
- Uncovered is the short puller
- Backside is thin: chop/sift the defensive end to second level
- Run off the ball when zone blocking. Great takeoff; use help to be aggressive
- Alert for line call adjustments (e.g., zone calls, blocking calls)

We use zone blocking rules. We try to have 18-inch splits. That is our normal alignment. Our back reads the end man on the line of scrimmage. He is keying the end man and based on what that guy does will determine if our back will cut it up inside or take it outside.

Is it a zone reach or tight reach? Following are our normal reach steps. If I am a guard with a 3 technique or a tight end covered with a 9 technique, I want to take the first step at an angle that will put my toes pointing outside of his outside shoe. My second step is to a point that is splitting his crotch. My third step has to establish leverage and gain something. Whether it is an inch, two inches, three inches, we would like to gain a lot. We want the third step to be upfield.

We have found from looking at our drills, the guys who can get their second step down with their seat going more north and south, the better chance he has of pushing up and through in order to drive the defender. He doesn't have to be perfectly aligned north and south going down the field. Once the defender starts to lose his leverage, the stretch is beginning to open up.

We want to take our inside hand and drive it through his down hand and drive it through his chest. We want to take his hand away from him as we go through our block. They always have their inside hand down. I want to drive my hand through his inside hand and pin it into his sternum. I think this technique is a big reason we were able to take our guys with short arms and dominate people at the line of scrimmage, because we take away their hands.

Now we move to covered without help, tight reach. Now, instead of driving the hand through the sternum, our hand is going to the near breast plate. We are not expecting any help to the inside, so we are expecting to drive the defender out. As he is fighting for position, we are going to let his momentum help us drive him out. He is trying to keep everything inside of him, so he is moving that way. We are counting on the running back to be able to read his block, and the end guy on the line of scrimmage.

Uncovered is the short puller. The short puller is literally checking out the near knee of the defender as he opens up. On his third step, he is deciding if he is helping on the covered defender or if he is working his way up to take on the linebacker.

Sometimes, the backside defensive end is a chaser. You may need to slow him down a little bit. By formation, we would like to keep the linebacker outside of the box.

We want to run off the ball when zone blocking. We have to know that we have help and we want to use it. Trust in your teammates.

We have to be alert of calls at the line of scrimmage. Sometimes, you might have a safety coming up and you have to go one man past. (Film)

This first drill is 1-on-1 where we were getting a lot of 3 techniques spiking (Diagram #1). When he gets off the ball, you want him to get his hands inside with a little leverage. I am looking to see if he gets his second step on the ground, splitting the crotch and is working and driving off of his insteps. I am looking to see if he can capture the arm of the defender as he come up into his chest.

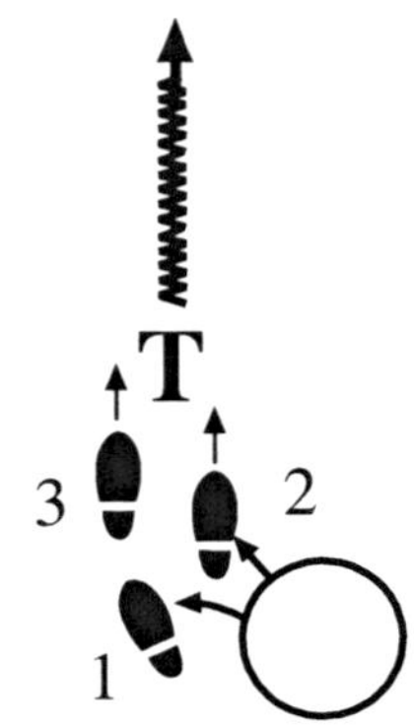

Diagram #1. Reach One on One

The next thing we go to is reach combos. You have to be able to short pull with the reach combos (Diagram #2).

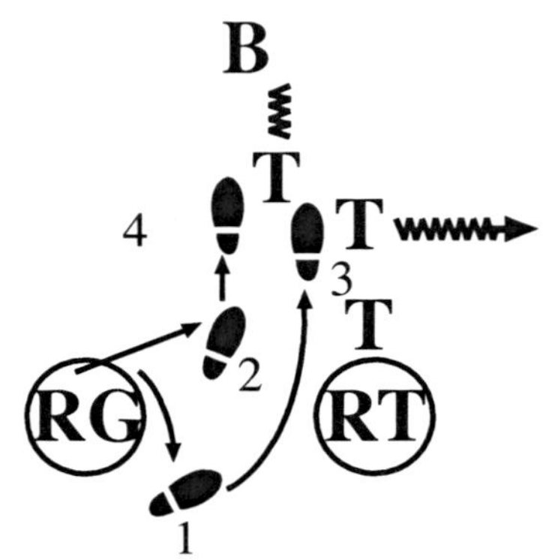

Diagram #2. Reach Combo: Short Pull

You will notice the right guard's first step is also pointed outside the down defender's outside shoe. This is where the short pull concept comes in. If the defender spikes inside, he will collect him. We want the tackle to keep his shoulders square and work up to the linebacker. If the down defender doesn't spike, the tackle has to stay on him long enough and then his shoulders square for the linebacker (Diagram #3).

Sometimes, the defense will be in a 4 or 5 technique. You have to be able to reach those guys. You are going to work on these combos hard for that week. On occasion, you will see our inside guy take his hand and push the outside guy off the double-team. That is a no-no. The tackle will leave the block when it is time to leave that block.

People ask me, "When is the proper time to leave the block?" The proper time is when you have to. First things first. We talk to our guys about taking care of the down defender first. First and

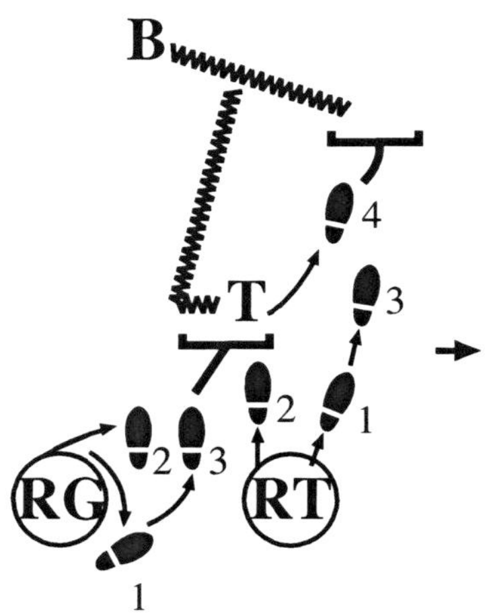

Diagram #3. Reach Combo: Scrape

foremost, take care of the down defender. When the down defender is secure, you can move up to the second level. You have to work it with the tight ends and tackles as well. You would like your helmet to the outside against the linebacker when he gets to the second level, just like on the down defender.

When we introduce a play in the springtime, we try to go with a set number of rules for the offensive line. For us, we go with three. These are the rules for our stretch.

Offensive Line Stretch Rules (2012)

- Covered/uncovered
- Take care of the down guy first.
- Zone run play

I will quiz our guys about their three rules throughout the spring. We can add tag words when variants occur. We can make adjustments for a one-back set or a two-back set. Sometimes, you want to run at a guy or away from a guy. We have different combo blocks to accomplish that. We would like to have rules that systematically carry over to the rest of our system.

The rules can change. These are the rules they came up with for this year.

Offensive Line Stretch Rules

- Outside Zone
- Two-Back Run
- Covered/Uncovered

Running Back Stretch Rules

- Aim point: One yard behind butt of tight end (ghost)
- Read key: EMLOS
- Stay tracks or vertical cut

(Film—Regarding outside zone play) You can run this from various formations. We will use the wildcat formation to run it. We are watching for the second step to split the crotch, especially when he knows he has help from the inside. It is all based on trust for that guy to cover that much ground. We can bring a guy in motion and hand it to him. We had to work on our timing when we bring that guy in motion quite a bit this spring. If he gets too close to the quarterback before the snap of the ball, you could really have something bad happen.

Openside 2 Back Stretch Rules

- Zone reach: Offensive line has 4 down to Mike and Sam; fullback has the Will
- If Will is on the line of scrimmage, make an "out it" call and block the Will. The fullback then will block the Mike.
- If the tight end is to callside, he will block force (corner or safety).

Now let me talk about the openside stretch. The fullback has the Will, but if the Will shows, we pick him up. If the Will is on the line of scrimmage, we will take the tackle out to the Will, we take the guard to the defensive end, and the fullback will adjust and get up to the Mike. Sometimes, we will motion the tight end to the side of the call if we get corners or safeties coming off the edge, and he will block force.

Single Back Stretch Weak Rules

- Offensive line to backside tight end must handle the box.
- Tag the play, and explain that the quarterback handles unblockable defender.

We have to handle what is in the box. If something is outside of the box, we can tag it with a pass or something to keep us out of harm's way and to allow us to continue to be successful. Don't call a bad play, let them know what the check is, and go with it.

Sometimes on the backside, the 3 technique will grab and hold on to us. We want to work through the defender's down hand as we move up to the second level. When we are in shorts, we will work on capturing that hand with our outside hand, from right off the ground on the first step. That causes the defender's shoulders to start to turn and allows the tackle to get in there and really push the defender downfield. We want to take away the hand of those grabbing defensive linemen.

We give our center the ability to pull if he needs to. If his man is a 20 technique linebacker, he may have to pull around in order to get him blocked.

With that, we have some variations that we have gone to as needed.

Variations of Scheme

- Tags/cages/badgers
  - ✓ Pin and pull concept
- Stops the flow of the defense
- Allows the tight end (or playside tackle in stretch weak) to attempt normal stretch reach and not tight reach. Thus stretching the defense!
- Combination rules still hold true but with different pieces
  - ✓ Still alert to Zorro Calls

Tags, cages, and badgers in our mind is the pin and pull concept. We also use these to stop the flow of the defense. If your are up against a really good 3 technique who is stopping up the B gap, let's take our tackle and go hit him in the mouth and try to slow him down a little bit. We could practice it both ways for the week and then in the third quarter decide "Hey, let's go ahead and tag it and get after him." The defense sees a different blocking scheme, but in our mind we are still running outside zone.

This is how we call our tags.

Cage: A combination block between the PSG and center. The PSG will block down and the center will pull around to get a better angle to the second level (Diagram #4).

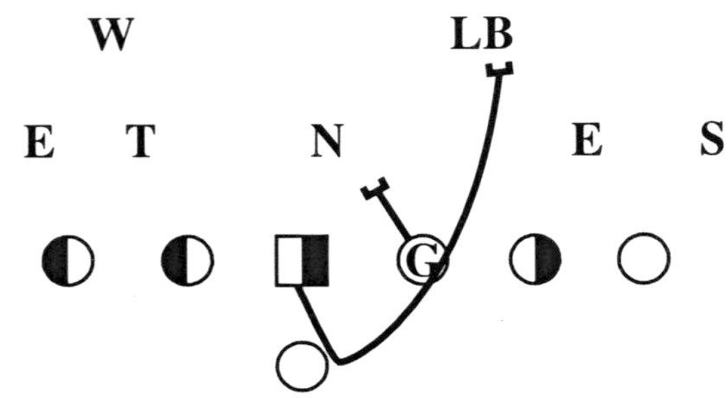

Diagram #4. Cage

We usually do not call cage with a 1 technique or a shade, but we have done it just to change it up. It is simple: center around the guard.

Tag: A combination block between the PSG and PST. The PST will block down, and the PSG will pull around to get a better angle to the second level (Diagram #5). Simple, tackle blocks down, and the guard comes around the tackle.

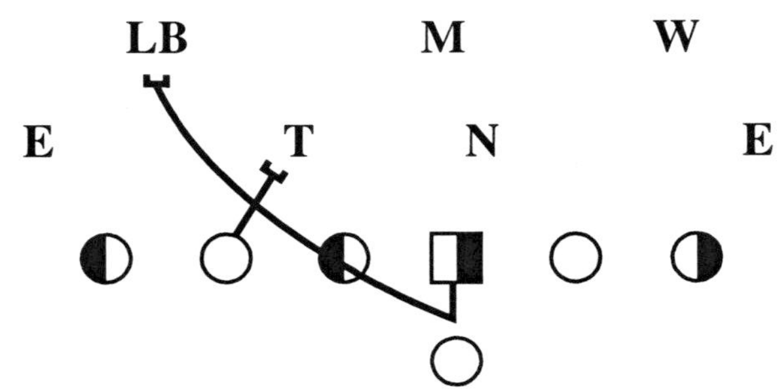

Diagram #5. Tag

Tex: A combination block between the PSTE and PST. The PSTE will block down, and the PST will pull around to get a better angle to the second level (Diagram #6). The tackle is coming around the tight end.

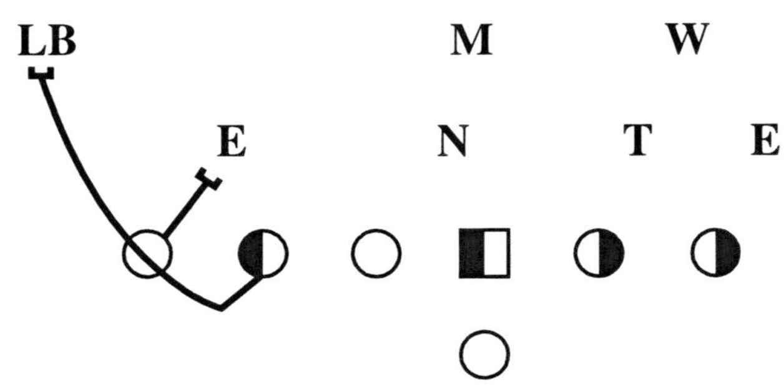

Diagram #6. Tex

Badger: A combination between the center and the backside guard. It is like a cage but on the backside; if there is a heavily shaded nose, the center will stay on the nose, and the backside guard will pull around to the second level. Must get depth to clear the tag block. We will often call a badger tag when we get a heavy nose.

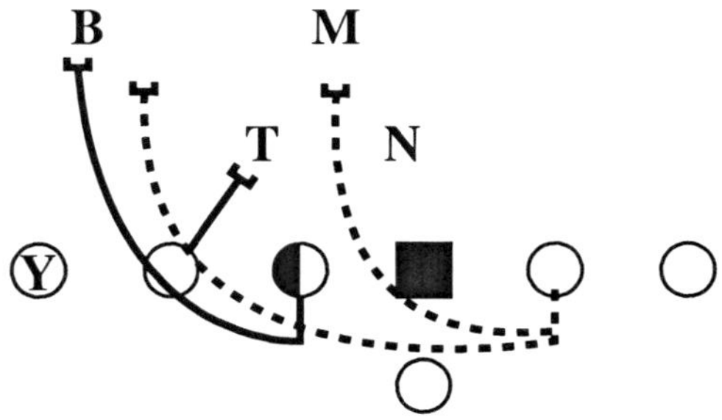

Diagram #7. Badger

Let me show some tape of our drill work with it. We start with some down blocks where we are trying to capture the near elbow. I want to see us pushing off of our insteps.

Next, we start working on the combinations. As we come to the second level, we want to continue to get our hat on the outside of the linebacker to give the back an opportunity to cut it to the outside if he needs to. Some guys like to pull with a front shoe lead, which I am fine with. Other guys like to skip pull with the back shoe first. You have got to play with what you got. The bottom line is: just get there.

The running backs know what we are doing. They are not clueless as to how we are blocking it. He knows where the cut could be.

We do not want to cut on the frontside. Why? Because your big ass ends up in the hole. Stay up if you can.

We have another adjustment where we cross block with the guard and tackle. This is against a 3 and 5 technique and a team that likes to close and feather down on the play and not come hard upfield. This is a good way to block it (Diagram #8).

The defensive end would come down and try to play it tight. Our guard will come around and hook him. It is a simple concept.

The last thing I have for you deals with picking up 5ers and 9ers.

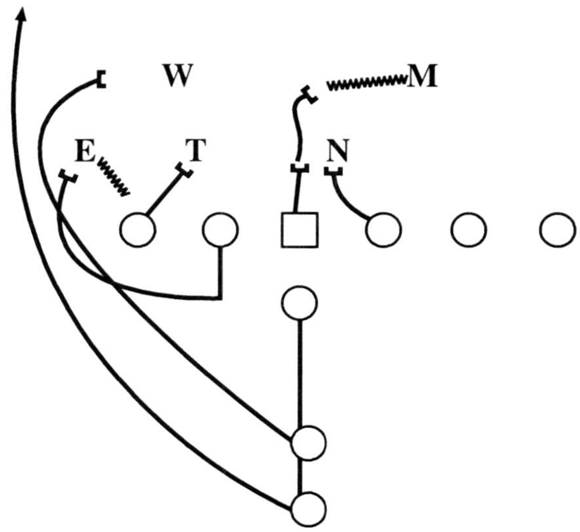

Diagram #8. Cross Blocking

Picking Up 5ers and 9ers With the Pin and Pull Scheme

- Center and playside tackle combo
  - ✓ Check the position of the defensive end on the track to the linebacker.
- Playside guard and playside tight end combo
  - ✓ Check the position of the defensive end on the track to the linebacker.

This is how we attack it. If we run 36, the tackle knows he can go after the defensive end because he knows if the defensive end spikes, the center is going to come around and pick him up (Diagram #9).

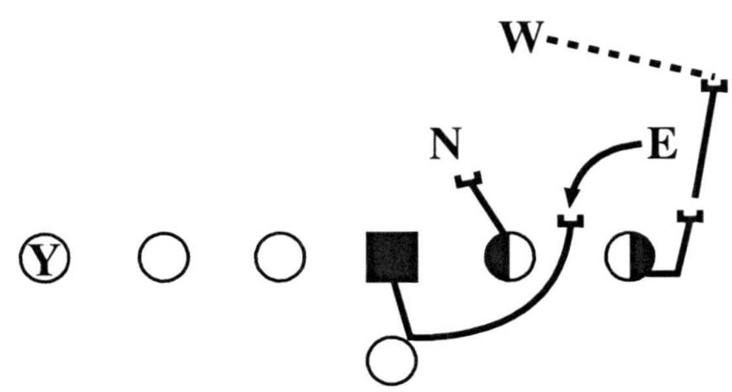

Diagram #9. Cage With 5er

The tight end can get after the defensive end knowing the guard has him on a spike.

I have a few clips on tape of us drilling it. If you are going to run it, you better drill it.

We have "rules of engagement" that we believe in and we talk about every day. They have to do with your players and how they are approaching what you are doing, how they are talking about what you are doing.

RULES OF ENGAGEMENT

Fully Engaged
Energy/passion
Innovative/loyal/good judgment
Become leaders

Moderately Engaged
Technically good/lacks inspiration
Contribution not as great
Frustrated about not being used

Not Engaged
Unhappy/not contributing much
Performance may decrease gradually
Discretionary time and effort is poor

Actively Disengaged
Ax to grind/working against you

- We cannot ignore the bear in the room.
- We are *all* at risk on different levels.
- Everyone therefore must have/add value.

I will be glad to answer questions in our group Q&A period. I want to thank you for having me here today.

ABOUT THE AUTHOR

Mark Staten just completed his seventh season on the coaching staff at Michigan State University and his third as the offensive line coach. He was promoted to offensive line coach in February 2011 after serving as the tight ends/tackles coach and recruiting coordinator for four years. Staten adds a mix of professional playing experience with a solid coaching background.

Staten helped mold the top offensive line in head coach Mark Dantonio's tenure in East Lansing during MSU's record-setting season in 2013. The versatile group, which saw as many as eight lineman in the playing rotation, was one of the main reasons why Michigan State continued to improve throughout the season on the offensive side of the ball.

All five starters received post-season recognition, including left guard Blake Treadwell (second-team All-Big Ten, coaches and media), center Jack Allen (second-team All-Big Ten, media), right tackle Fou Fonoti (honorable mention All-Big Ten), right guard Dan France (honorable mention All-Big Ten), and left tackle Jack Conklin (first-team Freshman All-American, Football Writers Association of America, *Sporting News*, and CollegeFootballNews.com). In addition, Allen and Treadwell were each named to the ESPN.com Big Ten All-Bowl Team for their performances in the Rose Bowl Game victory over No. 5 Stanford. Junior center Travis Jackson, junior guard Connor Kruse, and sophomore tackle Donavon Clark also were instrumental to the line's success.

For the third-straight season, Staten mentored a Freshman All-American, as Conklin earned first-team honors from the FWAA, *Sporting News*, and CollegeFootballNews.com. Allen was a first-team selection by the FWAA and *Sporting News* in 2012, while Jackson garnered Freshman All-American accolades in 2011.

Michigan State not only protected first-year starting quarterback Connor Cook, as the line gave up only 17 sacks (second fewest in Big Ten and tied for 15th fewest in the FBS), but it also paved the way for Jeremy Langford, who led the conference with 18 rushing touchdowns. When the game was on the line, the unit performed at its best—the Spartans ranked 16th in the FBS in fourth quarter rushing (56.8 avg.) and ranked seventh in the nation in time of possession (33:19 per game).

A four-year starter at defensive tackle at Miami-Ohio, Staten earned All-Mid-American Conference honors as a senior. He made the Cincinnati Bengals' practice squad as a free agent in 1993 before being added to the New England Patriots' roster for the conclusion of the 1993 season as well as part of the 1994 campaign. Staten was drafted by the World Football League's Barcelona Dragons in 1995, but sustained a career-ending knee injury.

Staten started his coaching career in 1999 as an assistant coach at Crespi Carmelite High School in Encino, California. He returned to Miami-Ohio in 2000 as a student assistant coach and was promoted to graduate assistant in 2001.

He graduated *cum laude* from Miami-Ohio in 2001, with a bachelor's degree in elementary education. In addition, Staten has started work on a master's degree in sports exercise science.

Staten and his wife Dana have two sons, Quinn and Maximus.

STATEN AT A GLANCE

- 2006—present: Michigan State University, Offensive Line Coach
- 2004—2006: University of Cincinnati, Tight Ends/Tackles Coach and Recruiting Coordinator
- 2002—2003: The Ohio State University, Graduate Assistant Coach
- 2001: Miami-Ohio University, Graduate Assistant Coach
- 1993—1994: New England Patriots, on roster
- 1993: Cincinnati Bengals, Free Agent
- 1989—1992: Miami-Ohio University, Defensive Tackle (four-year starter)

FSU STRETCH RUNS FROM DIFFERENT FORMATIONS

Florida State University

I want to thank my two graduate assistants for doing a good job with the slides and overhead material for this lecture. First is David Spurlock, who is our offensive line GA. Also, Matt McCutchan, who played center at the University of Kentucky, assisted with the technical aspects of the material I will present today. It is hell when you have a meeting at 6:00 a.m. and the only two people not there are the two GAs, right? They worked hard and came back and got in good graces.

Several of us were eating supper together this evening, and that was enjoyable talking with some of the older coaches. I think the football coaching profession is in good hands. I want you to know this clinic is one hell of a get-together. This is good for our profession.

I spoke at this clinic about six years ago. I never got a call to come back for several years. They invited me back after Florida State won the national championship.

Jim McNally, Paul Alexander, Bob Wylie, Dan Radakovich, Larry Beightol, Alex Gibbs, Jim Hanifan, Joe Bugel, and Dante Scarnecchia are the coaches that this clinic was built from. This is where the C.O.O.L., Coaches of Offensive Line, was built.

If you young coaches do not find you someone to latch onto and to study and follow and to gain the knowledge of some of the best coaches in the country, you are missing out on an important part of the game. For the Ohio guys, you have great coaches at Ohio State. You have more colleges in the state of Ohio than you have high schools. Find a college coach, or find someone you can turn to for guidance in your career.

I feel I should take my national championship ring and saw it in half and give half of it to Dante Scarnecchia of the New England Patriots. I get up early, and he gets up early. It got so bad last fall when I was driving into work at 5:30 a.m., I would call Dante. He would just pick up the phone and say, "Hello, Rick. What is up?" He knew who was calling him as soon as his phone rang. I had some problems this fall, and I found someone that could answer my questions. Any of the coaches I mentioned will help you if you just ask for help.

Coach Jim McNally and I were reminiscing about things we enjoyed. I go to church every Sunday because I need to go to church. However, before we get started, if one of those "F" words comes out, I am sorry. They are going to come out; I just do not know when they are going to come out. I do not mean to offend anyone. Those things happen when I get cranked up and get this lecture going.

We built a new addition to our church, and I have donated a lot of money for the project. After talking with Jim McNally for about two hours, I may have to go back to the church and make a big donation after this weekend. I know I cannot buy my way into heaven. I know the Lord is going to be looking down on me.

We were very fortunate this year at Florida State. We had a good year, and we had some good players. That always helps to have good players. We coach them as well. Our number-one run play is the split back stretch play. We run the split back zone, split back stretch, or whatever you want to call it. We run the split back power play. But we are going to run the stretch play. If you ask any player on our offensive unit what their number-one run play is, they are going to tell you it is the split back stretch play.

If you cannot say that, you are not going to have a very good offense. I think it is a great four minutes formation (Diagram #1). When we get into this set, I still have the following plays I can run from this set. I can run naked, inside zone with a cutter. I have the stretch play either way. We have a quarterback that can run from this formation. We can use the short passing game as well from this set.

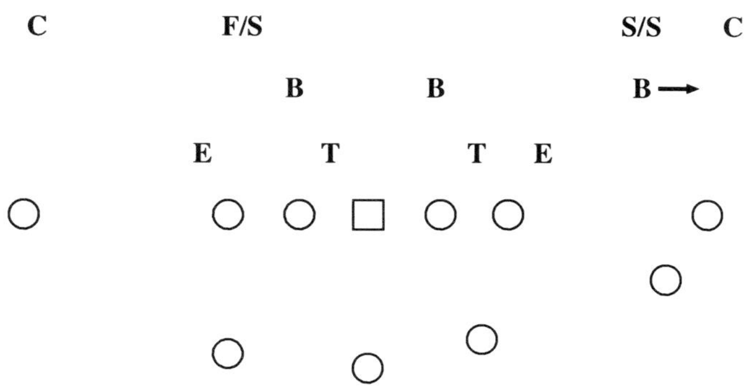

Diagram #1. Formation: Good Four Minutes Set

My guy believes in tradition. When we get into our four minutes plan, he wants to line up with two tight ends, with a flanker, and line up in the I formation (Diagram #2). They are going to run hippo down the stick, and they are going to have 10 defenders in the frame when we run that play. I do not like that. It makes it difficult to run the ball in this set.

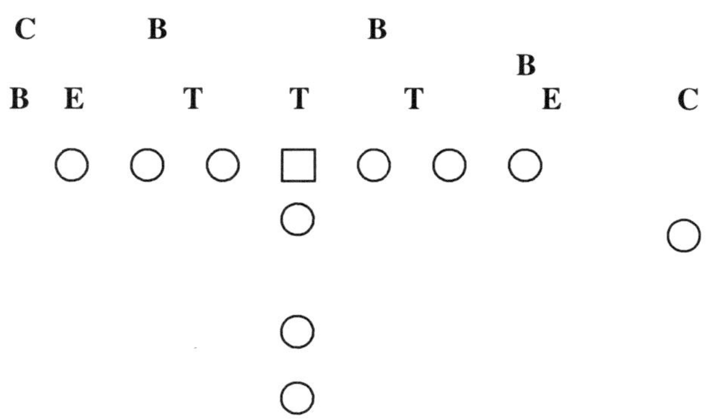

Diagram #2. Two Tight Ends/Flanker/I Formation

We do not have any runs that will work against this defense. If we get into the split set, we fill we have a better chance to be successful running the football.

I want to go over the stretch play and how we block it. I will show you the film so you can see how it works in a game. If I can get the overhead sheets straight, I can show you what we do. Those GAs did not draw the plays up where I could see how they have them drawn up. Here we go.

I know one thing about the stretch play. We run the play with the quarterback under center in the one-back set. If we see linebackers in the defensive alignment, I know we are going to get downhill linebackers coming to the fullback (Diagram #3). They are going to come downhill on you.

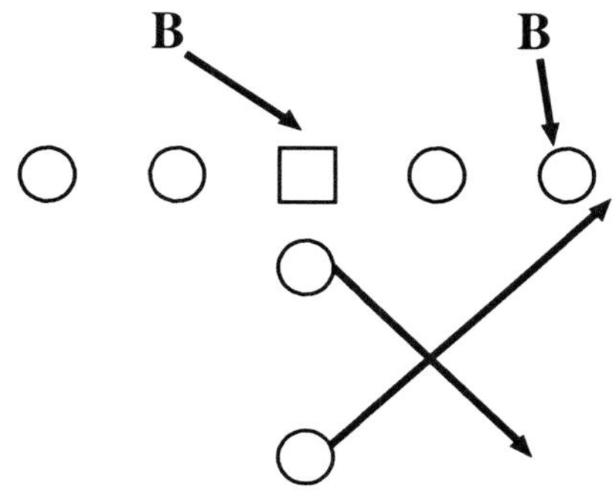

Diagram #3. Downhill Linebackers

The way we coach the play is like this: if we are in the shotgun, we want the backside running back to stretch his run so he arrives at the same junction point every time (Diagram #4). Not many of them are going to do that.

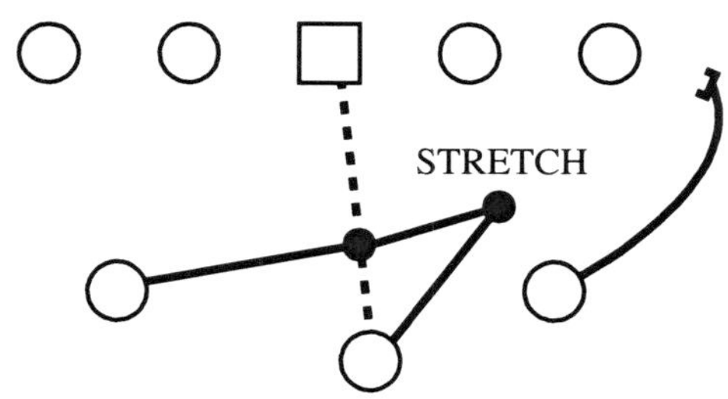

Diagram #4. Junction Point

The running back has to stretch the handoff to that same junction point. Problem area! When I say "Problem area," I can tell you what to look for, as I have been through this. If you are going to coach this play, this is what you must teach (Diagram #5). By the time the back gets the football on the stretch, he needs to know what the #1 read is doing. By the time he gets to the junction point, he needs to know what the #2 defender is doing.

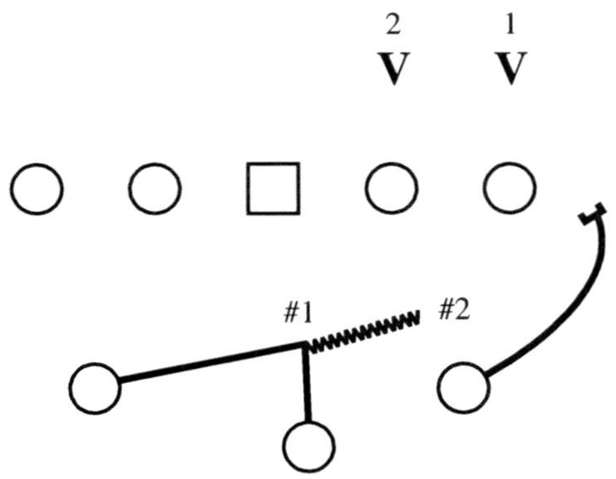

Diagram #5. Read Defender #1 and #2

I have been running this play for a long time. The longest plays in the history of Florida State football have come off this play. Two years ago, we had six touchdown runs of 70 yards or more. This was in one season, and they were all off this stretch play. Running back Chris Thompson was one of the reasons the play was so good. I like to think we had a little to do with the success on the play as well.

One other thing I have learned as well. If you run the stretch play and the ballcarrier runs across the designated path flat, the linebackers are going to pursue on a flat course (Diagram #6). The linebackers play flat all of the time. If you give me flat linebackers, I am going to whip someone's ass because they cannot do what they need to do against us.

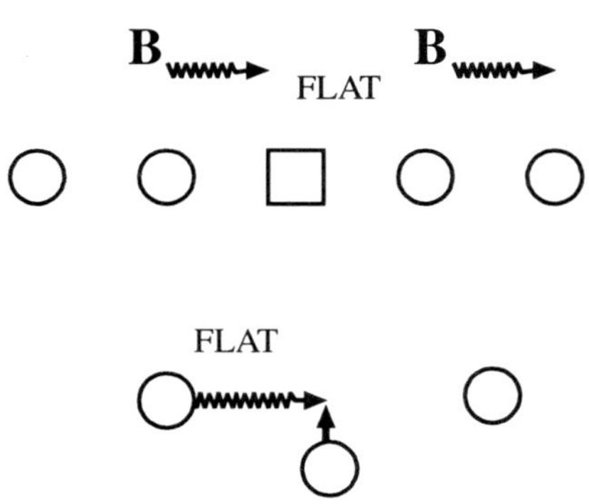

Diagram #6. Flat Path by Running Back

We have our guard split 18 inches from the center. We have two feet between the guards and tackles. The backs line up on the tackles at a depth of five yards (Diagram #7).

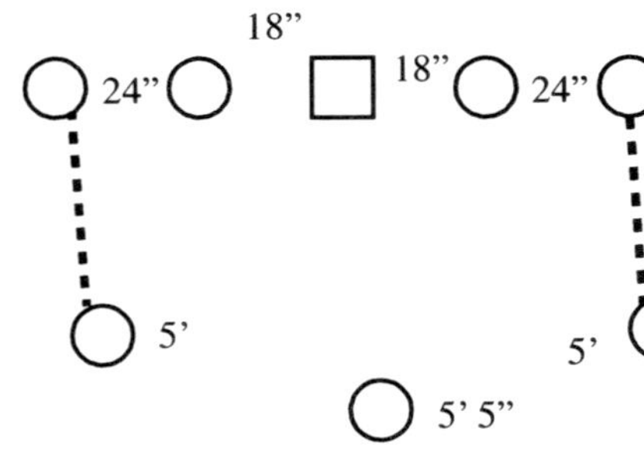

Diagram #7. Line Splits

A lot of teams run the no-huddle, the fast-pace offense, or whatever. The quarterback lines up at a depth of five and a half feet. The quarterback at a depth of five and a half feet. The quarterback lines up right beside the running backs' heels. If the running backs are deeper than five yards, it makes no difference to the quarterback. He still lines up on the heels of the running backs. That keeps his timing the same distance with the running backs.

- Regular rormation = F - H
- Pony formation = H - H
- Studs formation = F - F

We have different formations with the split backs gun set. First, we have regular (Diagram #8). We have the fullback in the left halfback position, and our tailback will be in the right halfback's position. That is a true fullback and a true tailback.

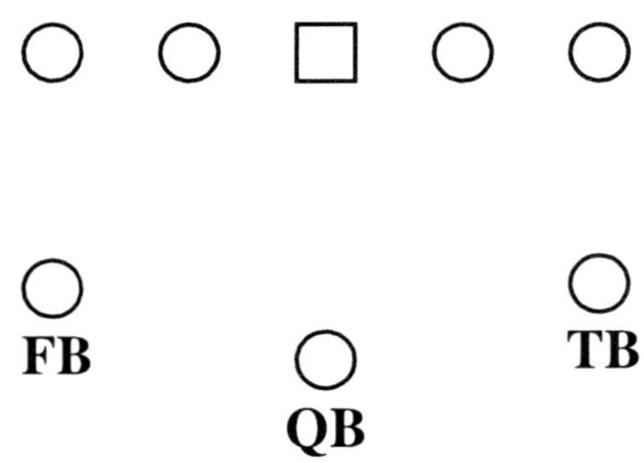

Diagram #8. Regular Formation

If we call for our pony formation, we want two tailbacks in the formation. If we call studs, we take the two biggest backs we have and put them in the running back positions in our four-minute offense. So we have three personnel groups with this play.

If we have the regular personnel group in the game, we have the fullback and a true tailback. If we call pony personnel, we have two tailbacks in the set. They are our fastest running backs. We want to stretch the play as wide as possible. If we call studs personnel, we have two big fullbacks in the game.

The traditional reads by the ballcarrier are the same. They still need to read the #1 defender at the handoff spot, and he needs to read the #2 defender at the stretch point.

I talked a lot with Alex Gibbs when I installed this offense when I was coaching at West Virginia University. When we started running the play, the running backs could read the #1 defender at the handoff spot, but when they read the #2 defender they looked at the linebackers. They made different moves to avoid the linebackers and made a lot of mistakes. We were not getting what we wanted out of the play.

We practice this play with the linemen and the running backs together. We run the stretch play against the defensive line only. We do not include linebackers in the drill (Diagram #9). The tackle comes off the ball and works outside. The guard reads the tackle on a pinch move. The back reads the #1 and #2 defenders. He stretches the play to the stretch point and then cuts it back inside, reading the blocking of our line. There are no linebackers in the drill. So the backs run the drill with the line and read the defenders without any linebackers.

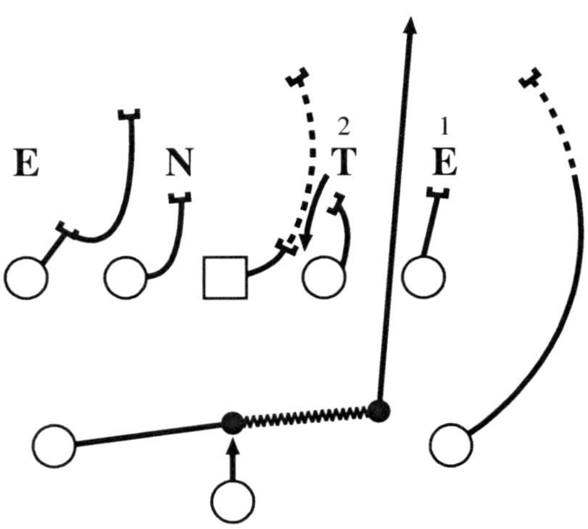

Diagram #9. Stretch Inside #2 Read

We work on reading the #1 and #2 read all day. We work the backside and run the angles to the linebackers.

If the #1 defender and the #2 defender go to the outside, we have the back break the play behind the center (Diagram #10). The back must read the defenders and make his cut at the stretch point.

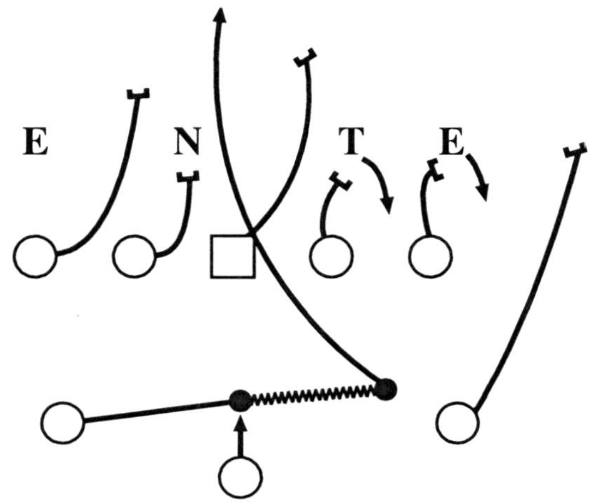

Diagram #10. Stretch Inside #1 Read

If the back reads the #1 and #2 defenders running a pinch move, he takes the ball outside (Diagram #11). We block it according to the two defenders the back is reading.

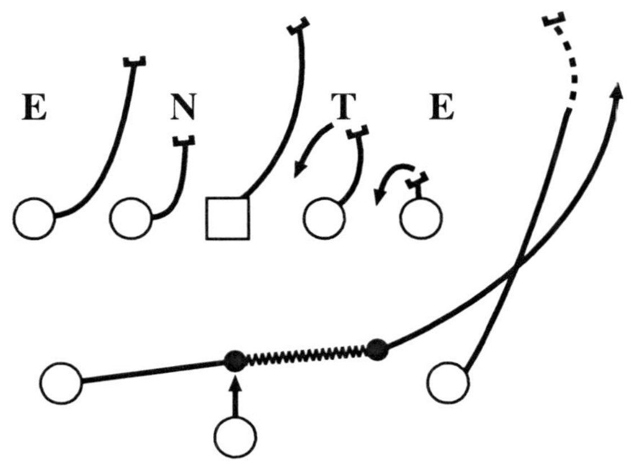

Diagram #11. Stretch Outside Read

We have three possibilities on the play. We have the #1 and #2 pinching. We have the #1 going outside, and the #2 man pinching. We have the #1 and #2 going outside. The quarterback hands the ball to the back coming across on the stretch. When that back gets the ball, he better know what the #1 defender is doing. He keeps stretching the play, reading the #2 defender. If that #2 defender goes outside, he is going to cut it back into the B gap.

The question is this: where is the point of attack? To me, the attack point on the stretch play is from the backside from the center to the backside guard and backside tackle. If we can get that backside shade, or the backside 1 technique cut off, we are going to gain yards.

I talked with some coaches in Orlando last night. One of them coached for a team we played last year. Before the championship game, they had told me there was no way we could get ready for that game and to do the things we needed to do against Auburn. They pointed out we could not get a scout team ready to show us what we needed to do to be successful. I just told the offense to haul ass and to run to the sideline.

This was my response to them. The stretch block for the linemen is nothing but a reach block. It is the reach block, cutoff block, and if a lineman is uncovered, he runs his angles technique. That is all the stretch play is for the linemen.

I tell our offensive line that we are going to execute the reach block better than anyone in the country. The first thing we do is to get them back off the football. We have our guard split 18 inches. He has his fingers on his hand on the ground between his shoestrings. He is back off the football.

If the 3 technique or the #2 defender comes forward, he is going to be reached. If he takes one step forward, he is going to be reached (Diagram #12). The defender better play the guard parallel, and he better be ready to move outside.

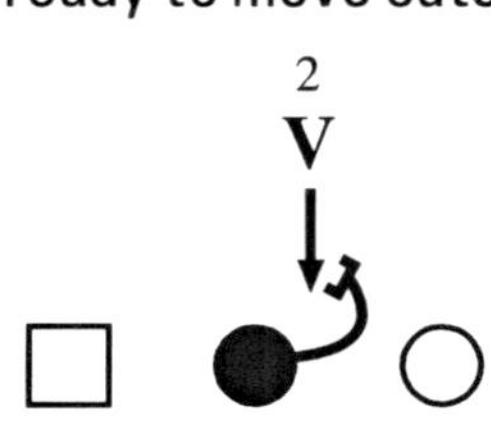

Diagram #12. #2 Steps Forward

Following is one thing I have learned in working on the stretch blocks when working with high school kids in our camps. As an offensive lineman, I am covered. I coach hard for the blocker to get his near shoulder over the defender's knee. The young kids I am coaching take the perfect step that I am teaching. But, they leave their shoulders back where they started from. They take the first step and keep their shoulders back in a parallel position. They end up a half step short.

I coach the second step as much as anyone in the country. I coach the hell out of that second step. My motto is this: "First step and then half placement step." If you do not get the first step down, screw the second step. I have to get the first step down.

If I am the tackle, I stretch, foot crotch, and bring my body through the block. We are coming off the ball and reach blocking the man outside. This is an aggressive play for us. We are stretching the play. I tell the blockers to go for the outside breast to the armpit. It is inside foot stepping to the crotch, outside breast, and tight elbows.

I am not sure if I have told this story before to this group. I went out to Iowa to visit the coaching staff. I spent more time with wrestling coach Tommy Brands and Dan Gable than I did with the football coaches.

You talk about techniques, the wrestlers use techniques quite a bit. They get down in a crouch position and use their hands to attack the opponent. All they talk about is tight elbows. If you have tight elbows, you have tight hands. If you have wide elbows, you will have wide hands.

So we coach the hell out of tight elbows. Tight elbows! Tight elbows! Tight elbows! We use the term so much I do not want to talk about it. We want tight hands, so I do not need to talk about it.

If our lineman is uncovered, when he stretches on the reach block, I want to bring my head and shoulders with me. It is a step, and then bang! I am talking about bringing the opposite shoulder over the knee as we make our move. When I do that, I have my hat on track, and then I can go with the block.

TEACHING THE STRETCH

Following is how I teach the stretch play. We will start working on this when we get back in school next week late May.

I bring the second-string tackle in the lineup, and I put him where the tight end would line up in a regular formation (Diagram #13). He is the unbalanced tackle over the tight end position. For this part, we do include the linebackers.

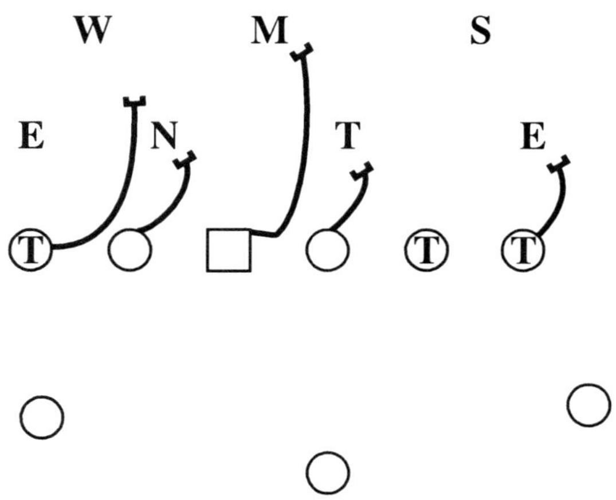

Diagram #13. Three Tackles in Formation vs. 4-3

Next, we show them a different look on defense. We have a 5 technique to the tight end side (Diagram #14). We have a shade technique on the center. On the backside we have a defensive tackle in a 4i technique. We have the linebackers in the picture.

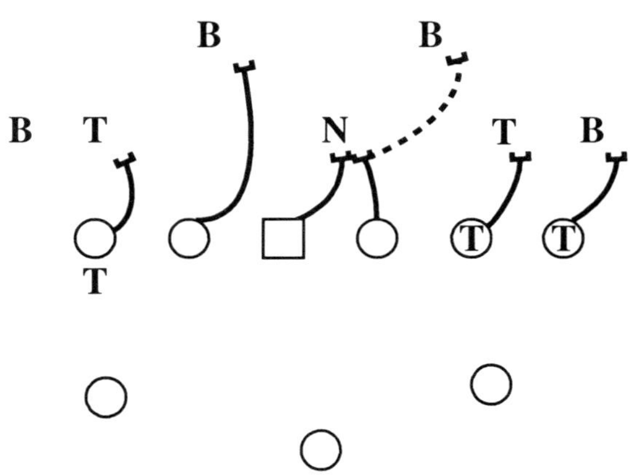

Diagram #14. Vs. 3-4 Defense

For three days, the line works against these two alignments. Stretch, work outside breast to armpit, and rip it. Stretch, work outside breast to armpit, and rip it. The backside guard has an 18-inch cutoff block against the 3 technique. The tackle has the 4i cutoff block against the 3-4 look. It does not matter if the linemen are covered or not. We want to make the game simple. What we do is to coach the crap out of the reach block.

When you do center-quarterback exchange drills, make them work on their blocks. My centers do 25 snaps per day on their own. When they do the snaps, they do not work on anything but reach blocking a 1 technique (Diagram #15). Every time they make a snap they are hooking a 1 technique. They reach the 1 technique. We do not reach block a shade or a gap. We reach a 1 technique.

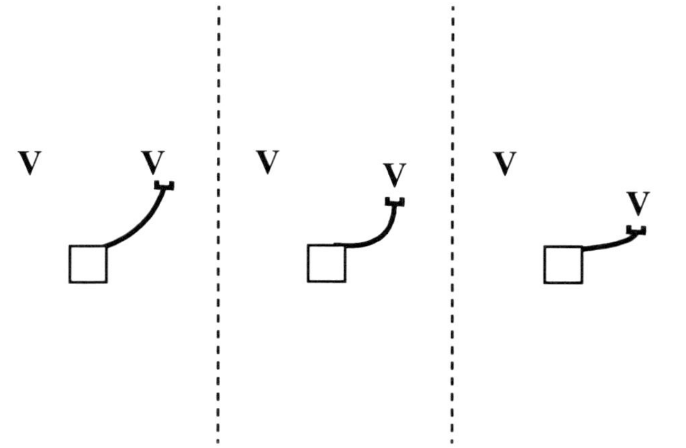

Diagram #15. Center Reach 1 Technique

After the centers get good at making the snap, and can reach that 1 technique. If we can reach block the 1 technique, we can hook the shade technique.

When I was at West Virginia University, I had a center by the name of Dan Mozes. He would look at the 1 technique in a game and tell him this: "You better move your butt, because where you are now, you are going to be reached." When he snapped the ball, he reached that man. The defender would move wider on the next play. Dan would tell him, "You better get wider than that."

When you get the players with that much confidence, you have a good player. I talked to Paul Alexander about this one time. I know this is a fact. When the center has to snap the football to the quarterback under the center, it is a much tougher block than it is when he just snaps it straight back to the quarterback in the shotgun. There is a difference.

For the snap in the shotgun, there is no handoff from the center to the quarterback. As the center brings the back up to make the shotgun snap, it is easier for him to step toward the 1 technique. You can get the jump on the 1 technique. All of my centers have learned to make that snap and the reach block. They have learned to get that little jump on the defender.

I had a center at Auburn that would come up to the line of scrimmage and he would flip the football, and he would gain six inches on every play. The officials would get on him for moving the ball up. He would spin the ball around and still move it forward six inches.

Following is what, as coaches, work hard on. If the lineman is uncovered, he runs his stretch move, and runs to the angle where the linebackers are. We stretch and run the angle of the defender outside of our alignment. I tell the defensive linebackers to haul ass and to move outside with the play.

We have a hard time blocking our defense. We get in a game, and the players will come out of the game and tell me, "Coach, the defense is not moving like our defense does." Let me tell you something. The cats we have to block are hauling ass and they move. That is a kind of good thing.

At times, we play teams where the linebackers are not as fast as we are used to seeing. I will tell Coach Fisher to hang with me for a series or two because I know we are going to be overreaching the defenders.

In the 4-3 defense, the tackles and center run the stretch and run the angle blocks toward the linebackers flowing toward the play (Diagram #16). They run the same technique and take off after those linebackers.

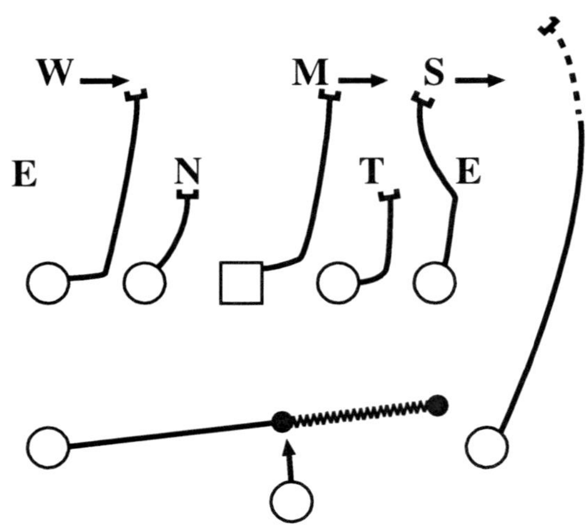

Diagram #16. Angle Blocks: Center and Tackles

We have everyone covered against the 3-4 defense, except the center and guards. The guards stretch and run the angle blocks (Diagram #17). The center reaches the noseguard. We want the guards to run those angles and get after those fast flowing linebackers. We do as good of a job of blocking that backside angle as anyone.

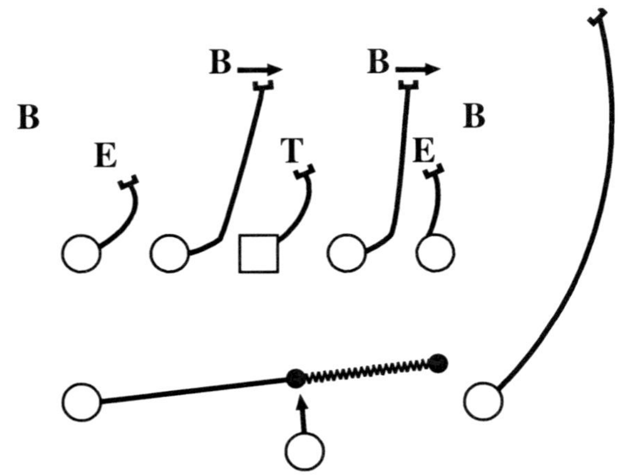

Diagram #17. Angle Blocks: Guards

If the 3 technique moves to the outside, the guard may have to grab grass as he goes through with his angle block. We tell the guard to think in this manner: "If the 3 technique is on the move, I am on the move." When the guard sees the 3 technique moving, he comes right off his butt. He grabs for the grass, and then feels for the linebacker.

We do not want them turning back and looking at the linebacker. When the lineman comes off the line on the angle, they must feel the linebacker, but I do not want them to turn their head and look at that linebacker. If the lineman turns his head back, you are going to end up with the backside defenders in the middle of the play every time.

I tell the backside guard to go toward the frontside linebacker to get the backside linebacker (Diagram #18). I tell the onside guard to run at an angle as if he is going at the safety on the strongside.

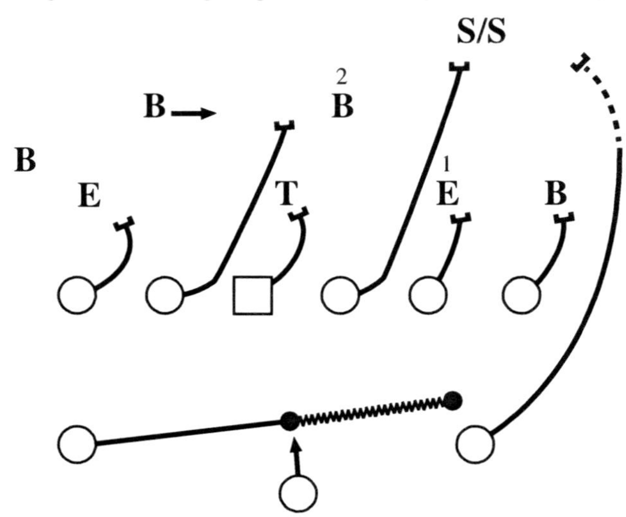

Diagram #18. Angles to Linebackers

We do a lot of bird hunting down in North Florida and South Georgia. I do not know a lot about bird hunting. I know when that bird comes up, and I aim at him and take a shot, that bird is still flying. If I lead that quail a little and then take my shot, I have meat on the table. It is the same thing with the linemen executing the stretch block at an angle. We want meat on the table. It is bang, bang, and bang.

Following is one point you need to know. This may answer the question just asked. We teach the lineman running the angle to read the defender's inside thigh.

I know some of you may be trying to run the outside stretch play from this alignment (Diagram #19). I am not going to run the stretch from that set. If the defensive lineman anchors up hard, we are not going to be able to get up to the linebacker.

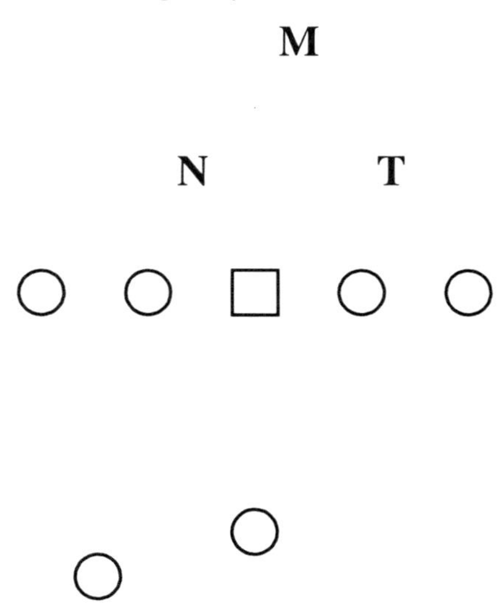

Diagram #19. Stretch: Offset Alignment

This is my feeling on banging it. If I am uncovered and I come off for the outside chest and armpit, and the 3 technique does not hit me in the mouth, then I can't get past the down man. I am avoiding getting to the linebacker. If I do a good job of reach blocking, there is going to be color.

The problem I have with this is: if I am the tackle and I have a 5 technique on my outside. Boom! I do a great job of reach blocking, and I have him hooked outside. I am on the outside breast, armpit. I have 75 to 25 percent of my body on him. I have him where I want him, and the head is outside. He is going to show color. I do not want to bang his ass. I want to avoid him.

I tell the backside men, or whoever is not covered, you stretch and show that near shoulder. If the defense does not hit you in the mouth by that time, then bang; go to the linebacker. Bang! You avoid him and get up there and go for the linebacker. We kind of scrape it off, but we are still going to the linebacker. We already have the 1 read hooked. I want to get the ball outside. I will get to that linebacker.

After we do the same blocks for three days, doing the base blocks with the angles both ways, we come back and add to the play for the next three days. I do the same drills off the 4-3 look, and the Okie look.

We are a multiple offense. We are going to run the one-back zone and the two-back zone. I have 21 combinations of pass protection schemes. I cannot get all of this coached the way I want to do it. However, I have been in the game long enough, and I have been in this system long enough to know what I have to get done. We have to get all of this done working against the 4-3 look, the Okie set, and the under defenses. Also, we have to work against the 50 defense. I can get all of the pass protections covered by working against the difference defensive alignments.

Next, we are going to one-gap the defenders (Diagram #20). We are going to do this for three days. We have to get it done. They know this, and I am not trying to screw with them.

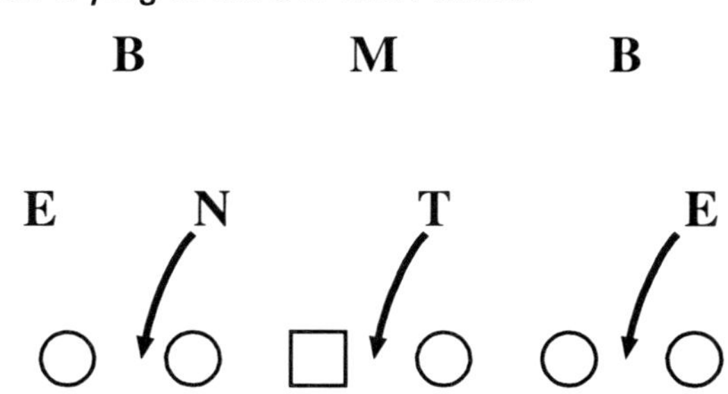

Diagram #20. One-Gap the Defenders

The guard works to the outside breast plate. The center reaches the 3 technique. This allows the guard to work up to the linebacker. We work that movement for three days. We work it out of the 4-3 look. When everyone has two or three snaps against the 4-3, we flip it over and run it back the other way. Then, we go to the Okie defense (Diagram #21). We

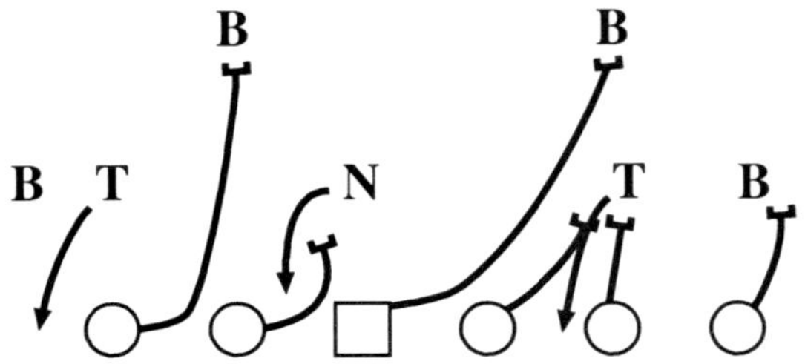

Diagram #21. Vs. Okie Defense

do the same movement out of this defense. We work against this look for three days.

I had a friend that had a horse that was amazing. That man could get the horse to do anything. I asked him how he got that horse to do all of the things he did, His reply was, this: "You have to have more time than the horse." All a horse does is eat and then take a crap. So they have all day.

We all get in a hurry in coaching. You should see our install program. By day three, it is *in!* We have a seven-day install. By day three, it is in. Teams want to throw a lot of different defenses against us. I believe in whole-part-whole. We never go back to "part." It is whole-whole-whole! I ask Jimbo and the offensive coaches, "When are we going back to part?"

The coordinators have their schedule, and I have my schedule. If a play does not work, we will get it fixed tomorrow. What I am saying to you is this. Don't be in a hurry. Get your part down and get the kids to understand what they are trying to do. After three days I will have the plays all scripted out. When we run the stretch, the offensive line will know what to do against the different defenses and the adjustments they make on defense. The defense may pinch, or they may widen. We will have a rep down for them to use.

This is the big one. We work our butts off on this—field south fire zone blitz. We are working against two-gappers (Diagram #22). We work against this look every day. The offensive line will get two reps on this every day. I do not want to brag, but I think we do as good of a job against the field south fire zone defense as anyone.

We work on this every day. They are going to get two reps on this every day. I was talking with Paul Alexander, and he said he remembered me saying I

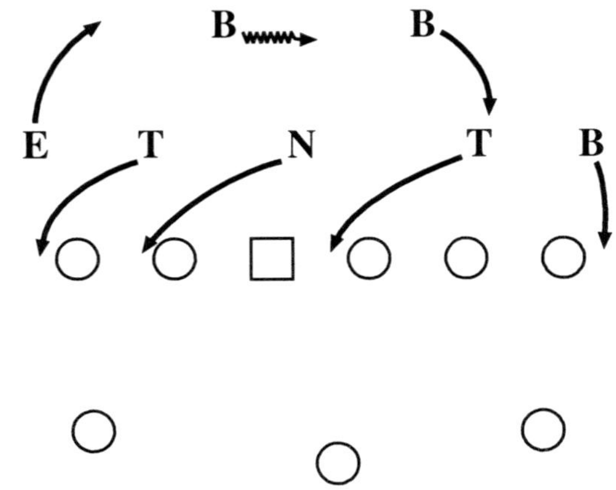

Diagram #22. Vs. Two-Gappers

was going to get 30 minutes of individual work with our offensive linemen when I spoke here the last time. Well, we are going to get 30 minutes with them.

I am on the practice field 15 minutes before practice begins every day. I want to work the linemen every minute I can get. Except for Friday, we are on the practice field Monday, Tuesday, Wednesday, and Thursday. I do not care what happens. We are doing two drive blocks, two reach blocks, and two cutoff blocks. We do these every day. Our saying is this: "Repetition is the mother of learning." To us, the base reps are what it is all about.

The problem area is a good coaching point. We tell our right guard, "Don't take the cheese!" (Diagram #23). The kids understand what I am talking about when I tell them that. The guard lets the tackle go, and goes upfield to the linebacker. The center will pick up the slanting tackle. If the guard picks up the tackle, you are screwed. That leaves the backside linebacker running free. So we tell that guard not to take the cheese, meaning not to block the slanting tackle. I will draw this up

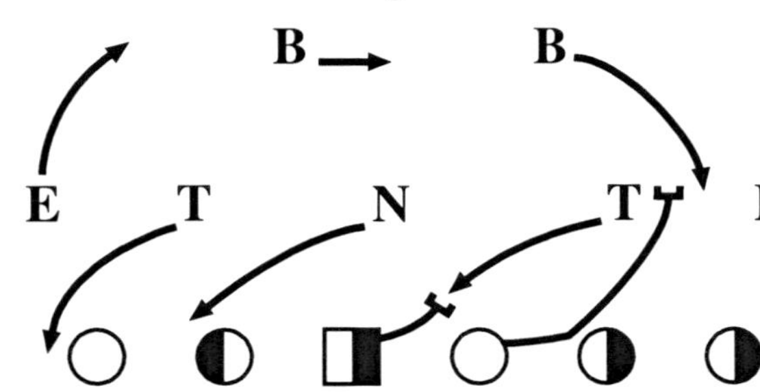

Diagram #23. Don't Take the Cheese

again for you. I see some of you have that dumb offensive line look on your face.

When we read the defense running the fire zone blitz, and we feel it is coming, we make a call all away across the board at the line of scrimmage. This comes from film study. We will take every field south fire zone the opponents run and watch it on film. That is all we watch. I do not watch base blocking with the kids. We watch all of the problem areas. We watch the field south fire zone blitz, cowboy corners, and all of that stuff. That is all we watch.

One thing I will tell you today. This is something I have learned in 42 years of coaching. On occasion, we bring Navy SEALs in to visit with our team. We had a couple of real wired up SEALs the last time we had them visit with our team. They were thereal deal. They were in on the Osama bin Laden raid.

They told our players they walked that mission over 100 times in his house where he was hiding. They could walk through that house blindfolded. "Eighteen steps here then turn right, go up four steps." They had it down.

I have a left guard who is a tough, smart football player. I can sit in the meeting room and talk on the board all day, and that guard will learn a couple of things. But if I can take him out on the field and walk him through the things I am teaching him, he has it down pat, and it will stay with him. He will never lose it.

I know everyone does walk-throughs. I do not meet much in the team meeting room anymore. If I have something we need to see, I am going to show it, and we are going to get it done. Then, we go out on the field and walk through the blocking, stepping through it, and running at full speed once we know what we are doing.

I have five seniors returning next year. Four of those five seniors were All-Conference last year. We have the two best guards in the country coming back next year. These players get bored at practice. They have been starting since they were freshmen. We took our lumps early. Then it all started paying off.

This spring, I moved our left tackle to center. I took the left guard and moved him to left tackle halfway through spring practice. Now I have a couple of rejuvenated players. It is tough for them to learn a different position. The tackle trying to learn the center's position is difficult. Now, he can't say that he does this crap every day. It is different for him. He has to make calls for the line as the center.

I took the right tackle and moved him to right guard. I moved the right guard to right tackle. Coach Fisher wanted to know what was going on. I told him to hang with me. I know what I am doing. We will be better tomorrow.

When you put players at different positions, and then when you put them back home, all of a sudden they know what they are doing. The tackles do not like going to the guard positions. I promise you that. You can write that crap down. The tackles that we moved to guard tell me, "Things happen a lot faster at guard." No crap! "If you think that is tough, try playing center." The tackles like it playing on the outside.

For the tackles, all they have to do is to know the simple rule of "man on, man outside." How complicated can that be? If there is no man outside, they go block on a secondary defender.

Following is what we tell our right guard. He is flat, and the nose tackle is flat. He steps toward the outside. He sees the defensive tackle slanting inside. We tell him not to take the cheese and not to block the slanting tackle (Diagram #24). He come over and lets the center pick up the slanting tackle. The guard rewinds and goes up where he can pick up the backside linebacker.

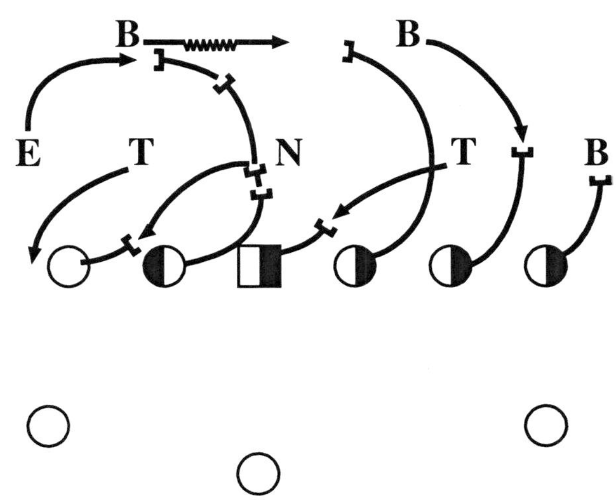

Diagram #24. Guards Block Linebackers

We tell the backside guard the same thing as we tell the frontside guard: "Don't take the cheese." He sees the nose man coming on a two-gap move. He is flat, and the nose is flat. He lets the nose go, and works up to the linebacker.

The tackle is on the outside chest to the armpit. He picks up the linebacker that is scraping on the play. The outside man takes the linebacker on the outside.

I pray that teams will run field south blitz defense against us. I remember playing Rutgers one year. That was when Greg Schiano was the head coach at Rutgers. They had just beat Pitt, and they ran the field south fire zone blitz about 60 times. They beat the crap out of the Pitt quarterback. They ran it one time against us and we broke the stretch play for 48 yards. He did it again and the stretch play went for 88 yards. I was over on the sideline yelling, "Run that fill south, defense." They did not run it anymore against us.

Our kids have confidence in hooking this blocking scheme up. To us, this is Biology III. Once you get past all of that other stuff, and your kids have confidence in what they are doing, they can become good at what they are doing.

Now we are going to watch the stretch play on video. I do not know how to turn the overhead off. If I do not have my GAs with me, we are not watching film. I have been doing this for 42 years. I am not learning all of the things they do on the computer. I am a damn ball coach. I can assure you I did not take the audio-visual classes in college.

To run this offense, we need two good tackles and a good center. I need a center that can hook up and run.

I will be around the rest of the night. If you have any questions, let me know.

ABOUT THE AUTHOR

One of the top and most respected offensive line coaches in all of college football, Rick Trickett enters his seventh season at Florida State and his 41st overall. He is nationally recognized for his ability to identify, recruit, and develop talent.

Trickett's standout offensive line group was vital to FSU's most productive offensive season ever in 2012 and 2013. The Seminoles set an FSU record with 6,591 yards of total offense and surpassed 500 yards of total offense six times behind a front line in which all five starters captured all-conference honors. Florida State rolled to its second ACC title since 2005 and an Orange Bowl victory. The Seminoles won the 2013 national championship defeating Auburn in the Rose Bowl.

In 2012, redshirt sophomore left tackle Cameron Erving (All-ACC Second Team) led the Seminoles to a victory in the Orange Bowl. Other outstanding linemen included redshirt junior center Bryan Stork (All-ACC Second Team), sophomore right guard Tre' Jackson (All-ACC Second Team), junior Menelik Watson (All-ACC Honorable Mention), and sophomore left guard Josue Matias (All-ACC Honorable Mention).

In 2012, Florida State ranked second in the ACC in rushing offense (206.21) and third in total offense (471.50) and scoring offense (39.29). In the nation, FSU was 24th in rushing offense, 19th in total offense, and 10th in scoring. The Florida State offensive line allowed EJ Manuel to wrap up an impressive career as he passed for 3,392 yards and 23 touchdowns en route to All-ACC Second Team honors. Manuel was the first quarterback selected in the 2013 NFL Draft (16th overall) by the Buffalo Bills.

In addition to Manuel, Florida State's running backs enjoyed tremendous success in 2012. The Seminoles' rushing attack by committee produced a new school record for rushing touchdowns with 40 and tallied 2,882 yards on the ground at a 5.6 per carry clip. Senior Chris Thompson (687 yards, five touchdowns) and sophomores Devonta Freeman (660 yards, eight scores) and James Wilder, Jr. (635 yards, 11 scores) all eclipsed the 600-yard mark, while senior fullback Lonnie Pryor added eight touchdowns, and Manuel produced four scores. FSU's front line proved it could open holes for anybody as an unprecedented five different Seminoles rushed for 100 yards or more in a game, capped by Pryor's 134-yard, two-touchdown MVP performance in the Orange Bowl.

FSU's lack of experience on the offensive line made the 2012 season's success even more impressive, as only Stork had more than one start among the front five heading into last year's campaign. Erving spent his first two seasons as a defensive lineman before switching to offensive line, while Watson, a former collegiate basketball player from Manchester, England, had never played a down of NCAA Division I football. Jackson and Matias picked up their first starts against Notre Dame in the 2011 Champs Sports Bowl.

Trickett was able to turn a question mark into an FSU strength in 2012 and helped develop Watson from an unknown prospect into a second round pick (#42 overall) by the Oakland Raiders in the 2013 NFL Draft.

Heading into 2013, FSU will break in a new quarterback, but the front five will be arguably the Seminoles' strongest and most experienced group with Stork, Erving, Jackson and Matias returning as entrenched starters and senior Jacob Fahrenkrug (12 career starts) and juniors Austin Barron (three career starts) and Bobby Hart (nine career starts) capable of making an impact.

At Auburn, he coached four linemen—Wayne Gandy, Willie Anderson, Victor Riley, and Kendall Simmons—who were selected in the first round of the NFL Draft.

More than 30 players Trickett has coached have gone on to play in the NFL, and more than 35 players have won all-conference honors, including four of his five linemen at West Virginia in 2005 and 2006 and all five Seminole starters in 2012. At LSU in 2000, three of his players earned All-SEC honors.

Trickett earned his undergraduate degree in 1972 from Glenville (WV), where he was an all-conference strong safety. He received his master's degree from Indiana (PA) in 1975. Trickett is a U.S. Marine Corps and Vietnam War veteran.

Trickett released a book in 2012. *Complete Offensive Line* is a comprehensive guide to the techniques, drills, and game strategies necessary to develop an effective offensive front.

The Tricketts have been a fixture on the FSU campus since Rick's 2007 arrival in Tallahassee. Two of Tara and Rick's sons have been involved in the football program with Travis serving as an offensive graduate assistant in 2010 after serving as a videographer. He received his master's degree from FSU and is now the co-offensive coordinator and quarterbacks coach at Samford University. Clint spent three years as a quarterback for the Seminoles and graduated with a degree in social science. He will continue his football and academic career at West Virginia in 2013, and 2014 this fall. Chance graduated in spring 2011 with his bachelor's degree.

Tony Wise

PASS PROTECTION CONCEPTS, TYPES, AND TEACHING

NFL Alumni

I want to talk about a schematic approach to pass protections, calls, and adjustments. I have been asked, "What is your favorite protection?" There is not a favorite protection. I want to know who they are bringing. Are they bringing the Will? Are they bringing the Sam? Are they a zone blitz team? We are going to have in the offense whatever we need in order to get them blocked.

This is not rocket science. Norv Turner and I did not want Emmitt Smith to have to block somebody so whoever they were bringing, we were going to have our linemen block on them. So there is no "favorite protection" to call. I do not want to tell my guys we have 20 different pass protections either. I want my guys to learn concepts. I want to have a core group of protections in the offense. That is what I want to talk about today: concepts.

We have seven different pass protection concepts. You may say there are more, and you are probably right, but I do not want my players to be thinking about a whole slew of protections. I want them thinking conceptually based on the play call.

We teach concepts, not five-man, six-man, or seven-man protections. I want them thinking we are in an empty backfield with no blockers back there. I want them thinking gaps. I did not say to them in a meeting, "We are putting in five-man protection today." We would talk in terms of gaps and where help was going to come from.

Do not change protections from week to week. As offensive line coaches, we have to work alongside the offensive coordinator. If he sees the opponent likes to bring the corner, he might ask if we can change the schemes. No! Why? Because it leads to too many busted assignments, easy sacks, and pressure. The worst thing to do as an offensive line is to allow a sack because somebody didn't know they had the sacker. If a defender whips somebody because they are a better player, we can better understand that.

Changing schemes also prevents the line from getting better through repetition. Obviously, on critical downs, we need perfect execution. In the final two minutes and the score tied with third down and eight yards to go, they have to know without a doubt what they are doing.

We want the terms in the schemes to allow the linemen to know the depth of the drop for the quarterback. In your offense, is there a word that alerts everyone that the quarterback will drop to three steps? I think it is extremely important for the offensive tackle to know it is a three-step drop so he can make the appropriate block to get the defender's hands down for a three-step drop pass. He needs to know that the ball is coming out quick.

We also want to know where the quarterback will be throwing from and with deeper routes, how much time we will be required to protect the quarterback. In our case the D's were the deeper routes. Dig, Dino, and Dagger for example. In other offenses it may be by the play number such as a 9 or 4 series. If it is a quick pump and then throw on a double move, it is important for the linemen to know that.

Terms in a scheme that indicate what type of play-action is important. I know I am being redundant. I can't help it. A 4 series might mean play-action. 432 is play-action. The players on the offensive line need to know and understand that and the concepts of blocking for that type of play.

Is this going to be a hard sell type of blocking? Do I need to keep my shoulders down to confuse the reads of the defense?

Put a tag onto an existing protection such as play pass, base, or show. These were words to indicate this is play-action protection. Again, what type of play-action protection is it? Is it a hard-sell quick pass, or is the quarterback going to hold the ball a little longer and try to hit something down the field? The players need to know what type of play-action and what we are expecting when we do that.

The strength in any protection is the ability of the line to make an adjustment quickly because they have had repetition of protection. In the places I have been around, we had blitz drills we used in practice to learn to execute under pressure. We had to recognize the blitz and make the right calls to execute our protection of the quarterback. I always liked to work on pressures in team periods. I would especially recommend you do this in your early practices and in spring ball. I know a lot of the uptempo guys might not feel as strongly about that, but I always thought it was important. I would go to the defense coach and ask for him to give us some pressures during our team period for the day.

We all need to go back and remind our coordinators and head coaches that pass protection is a group effort, not just the responsibility of the line. I had a great working relationship with Norv Turner. He would tell everyone that it was a team effort. We know as line coaches we got to get them blocked. The receivers have to run their routes with the proper timing. When the back is called on, he has to step up and make the block. If the quarterback is asked to deliver the ball on the fifth step, that is what he has to do. We have to have a sense that we all have to work together to get the play run properly. It is not just the offensive line.

Getting back to concepts, you should teach concepts both from an offensive standpoint and from a defensive standpoint. The substituted player is the nickel Will linebacker or Sam linebacker. Be prepared to count or designate a rusher by use of number. On third down, one of the opponent's linebackers may be an excellent rusher. The defense may line him up on the edge or walk him up. We may go into a game with the idea that on third down we are going to identify number 48 as a rusher regardless of where he lines up.

Now we call the front accordingly with an over or under. Even though 48 may be in a 20 technique, we will make a call and consider the guard covered because we know through film study, he is probably coming. We then block it accordingly. I'll be more specific here in a second.

The center's "point" and "I.D." is critical. I am a fan of having the guy that studies all of the defensive fronts to make the call. I want the center to make those calls. Some quarterbacks aren't as talented as Tom Brady in that area.

Try not to invent a protection. Once we have our base concepts, we want to work within those concepts. We have specific terminology we use for a given situation. We do not want to come up with something new that we have to learn.

As I said earlier, our protection schemes must be concept-driven. The players must understand that all passes are not the same. I think the kids get to the point that if we are throwing the ball, all the blocking is the same. It is not the same, as we know. As an example, in base protection, we have the four down linemen and the Mike. The backs have the outside linebackers.

In slide protection, we have the four down linemen and the Sam or Will. The halfback will double read for the Mike or Sam. We could slide in either direction. In burn protection with two backs, we have the four down linemen and the Will or Sam. The halfback and fullback have the Mike and outside linebacker.

In a game, if they show an all-out blitz, we should have a tool to help us deal with that. We should have a gap protection call that we can go to in that situation. The linemen, tight end, and fullback have a gap that they are responsible for.

In flood protection, we have the four down linemen, Mike to Sam. The halfback or fullback has the outside linebacker away from the call. In empty protection, we have the four down linemen and one linebacker either strong or weak. In today's offense, this type of protection is more prevalent.

These concepts can fit any personnel, group, or formation. These protections can be used as a play-action scheme with the appropriate tag.

At the line of scrimmage, the center calls the front. We are going to call the front every single time. Odd, even, over, under, or bear. There is information in that call that we are going to give out to everybody. We study all of this film to determine how they like to operate and what their tendencies are for a given look. When we make a call, everybody's mind should click to know what to expect from that given front. That is huge.

The center is going to point out the linebacker. This puts the line and the quarterback on the same page. I know some quarterbacks make the call, and I do not necessarily disagree with that as long as we do it quickly. We do not want to stand over the ball and do a bunch of pointing all over the place. Make the call, put your hand down, and let's go to work. Remember, everyone must hear the front call and be aware of the point.

When we line up against a walk-around front, we want to identify the number of rushers. If a defensive lineman is on or off the line of scrimmage, we determined him to cover one of our offensive linemen. The center makes the call for that.

Let me get into the different types of protection.

BASE PASS PROTECTION

- Line has four down and Mike linebacker; double fan or solid (fan versus 3-4)
- Backs have outside linebackers on their side
- Used to be sound versus pressure
- The backs can help to either or both sides.
- Used on deeper routes
- It can be adjusted versus secondary pressure, new Mike call
- Calls: solid, heavy, fan, gang

SLIDE PASS PROTECTION (TWO BACKS)

- The line slides to first defender away from the call or backs.
- May include the corner
- Quarterback is deeper because of action fake
- Called strong or weak (term)
- Can be two-back draw action
- Backs have Sam and Mike or Will and may interchange assignments by change in term (fox, hound, or number 4, 6)
- Can be adjusted versus secondary pressure or to ensure a back releasing
- Calls: (fan-open) (Ray-LB), heavy, money
- Techniques: emphasize not going too far
- Guards protect inside when center goes away

The biggest thing you are going to see on film for slide protection is we are going to slide and make them come to us. We are not going to over slide. We are going to slide and get tight.

What is critical with every protection we will cover is to set away from your help. If I have help from the center, I am going to set half a man on the defensive tackle. I want to get my eye outside as the center comes to me. If I am the right guard and the center is sliding away from me, I must get inside leverage on the defensive tackle so I protect the center that is going away. Know where your help is and set away from your help.

DOUBLE READ PROTECTION

- Line has four down linemen and the most dangerous of Mike or Sam
- Versus 3-4, guard-tackle away from call block outside linebacker and defensive end
- Back to call has a "free release" and runs his route
- Back away from call has linebacker to his side to corner
- Scan term has been added for halfback to scan across to short safety
- Will throw "hot" versus some pressures
- Can be adjusted versus secondary pressures
- New Mike call
- Ball will come out quicker
- Calls: solid, rob/low, heavy, fan, sort
- Techniques: Slide technique versus Sam off line of scrimmage
- Full technique versus guard bubble
- Sort technique versus even Sam

EMPTY, GONE, OR NO-BACK PROTECTION

- Line has five most dangerous rushers
- Used to create easy or quick throws for the quarterback
- May slide and protect backside or frontside of quarterback
- Must be aware of point to protect against inside pressure, frontside guard and tackle be ready to gap
- May be adjusted to take advantage of coverage or pressure
- Tackle assesses the defender on slot wide receiver or safety, determines threat, remain in slide or center reacts to call and changes to dual opposite direction
- Be aware of backfield set or empty, linebackers will give it away
- Calls: off, fan, Ray/Lee, rob/low
- Ball will come out quickly

We want to emphasize to the players that the reason we are in empty is the quarterback is going to have a quick throw with everybody spread out. He is going to pick strong or weak, and the ball is coming out. We are not going to drop back and throw a deep crossing route. That is not the point of this protection.

When we make a call and call out the Mike, the away side has to understand that there isn't anyone behind them to help protect the quarterback. That is what I mean about understanding concepts. They have to know if a man walks up in their gap, they have to get them blocked. There is no other alternative.

ADDING THE TIGHT END TO THE PROTECTION AS A BLOCKER

- Allows formation flexibility to a protection
- Tight end on or off line of scrimmage
- What is the ability of the tight end?
- Always remember tight end's limited practice time as a blocker
- Have a number term to add to protection:
  - ✓ Changes responsibility
  - ✓ When uncovered, tackle will set then help the tight end
  - ✓ Tight end, make call leaving the huddle

It is always important to evaluate the tight end as a blocker. He is not spending as much time practicing his blocking in pass protection as the interior linemen do.

HELP ON THE EDGE

- Three techniques that were used:
  - ✓ Chip by the back or tight end on edge or rusher from off line of scrimmage, route is run
  - ✓ Hit or collision by back or tight end on rusher from off or on line of scrimmage, no route is expected to be run
  - ✓ Bluff or chip by tight end or wide receiver on the move, any motion can be used, route is run
- One of the most important aspects is choosing terms that convey to players exactly what is expected:
  - ✓ Chip, crunch, crush, blast
  - ✓ The tackle is being helped, the halfback is not blocking the defensive end
  - ✓ Tackle has to hear the call
- Be aware the defensive end will see the help and may rush accordingly, as game goes on and he sees plan he may go inside sooner
- Backs never take their eyes off their linebacker
- Practice to get angle, and tackle senses how hard it is
- Give various movements of defensive end so halfback can react and get out

This was kind of fun in that it was a little creative in determining what we were going to do to help on the edge. Hey, we can run the route from there if we need to bring someone in motion to help out on the edge.

ADJUSTING THE PROTECTION

- Adjusting a protection by declaring a different linebacker responsibility—commonly called "New Mike"
- This is a concept that can be used in most protections, if desired, when the defense has tipped their hand to a specific pressure.
- The quarterback points out the number of the linebacker one over from the line's responsibility, making that linebacker the "New Mike."

- A direction can be given, but is redundant.
- Backs see "point" and block their new assignment
- Line reacts and uses any appropriate calls
- Teach concept that the quarterback is adjusting protection for a reason ("Here they come")
- Do not restrict the quarterback; he must have the freedom to call it.

The point is when we adjusted the protection to a "New Mike" was because they were blitzing. That is the concept with this. It is not as though we are guessing. They are giving it away, and the quarterback is going to make the adjustment to make it easier to block.

I want to make a quick point. When we are talking about a defense and responsibilities, we want to be specific. A backer is not a backer. He is the Sam, Mike, or Will linebacker. I did not allow certain words such as maybe, like, and "kinda." I want them to be specific. What kind of front is it? Under! That is specific.

In the first meeting we have for the upcoming game, I let my guys know what the base front will be. I tell them something like 3, 1, and 5 techniques with the Sam on the line of scrimmage. I want them to understand the opponent's base front. That alerts them that anything different from that alignment, there is something going on. The defense is up to something.

PREPARATION VS. LINEBACKER AND SECONDARY BLITZES

- Recognition and anticipation are keys:
  - ✓ Alignment changes
  - ✓ What do they like out of what front (scouting reports)?
  - ✓ Area of the field or down-and-distance
- Communication
  - ✓ Line calls: simple, loud
  - ✓ Line to the backs: exchange of assignments
- Be physical versus linebackers and safeties.
- Do you need to limit protections versus certain opponents?
- Make adjustments consistent and conceptually driven:
  - ✓ Do not cause indecision with difficult adjustments
  - ✓ Try not to break rules
- Practice at full speed: blitz drill
- Make them run the pressure correctly; you cannot run two defenders in the same gap.

TEACHING PASS PROTECTION

We do things a little differently than some other guys. We get up on the line of scrimmage and crowd the ball. Our hands are at the back tip of the ball. We do not want to give those guys one inch.

When the two guards and center have slide protection, they have to know where their help is coming from (Diagram #1). If they slide to the right, the right guard will not get beat to the inside because the center is sliding over to help. He must protect the gap to the outside.

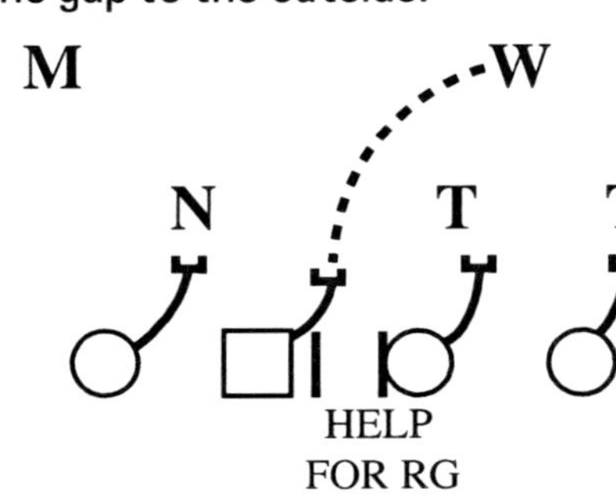

Diagram #1. Slide Protection

Against a solid look, the right guard has inside help. The center will set away from his help so he sets to the right. The right guard sets to his right, away from the center. The right guard cannot let the defensive tackle beat him to his outside. If the tackle slants, he has help from the center. The center is looking for the linebacker. The left guard has to get inside leverage.

I want to make a point. Linebackers have spent no time rushing the passer while in practice. They may have has some little drill where they come one hundred miles per hour, trying to whip a back. They really have no skill versus the offensive line, when rushing the passer. We emphasize to take on the linebacker and get our hands on him and get him locked out. He has no skill rushing the passer. We talk about that.

We go into every week with a game plan. We want to know who we are helping on. If 93 is all-league, every chance we get we want to help on 93. We want to know ahead of time who the guys we are helping on. In this case, the right guard was going from Mike to Sam. They don't come. We want him to get back inside and drill the noseguard, number 93. When we help on someone, we are going to drill them.

Guys, it has been a pleasure. Thank you very much.

ABOUT THE AUTHOR

Tony Wise, an accomplished 37-year coaching veteran of collegiate and professional football, recently retired in 2011 after finishing his third year at the University of Pittsburgh as their offensive line coach.

During his first two years at Pittsburgh, Wise's offensive line was instrumental in helping the Panthers' average 32.1 points per game last year, one of the top five scoring averages in school history. The Panthers gave up only 1.15 sacks per game, tops in the Big East and 16th nationally. Moreover, Pitt's offensive front paved the way for the country's No. 3 rusher in Dion Lewis (138.38 yards per game). Lewis's total of 1,799 yards is the second-highest single-season total in Pitt history. Under Wise's guidance, guard John Malecki and tackle Jason Pinkston were first-team All-Big East honorees in 2009. Pinkston was also named a second team All-American by SI.com and Rivals.com. In 2008, Pitt's offensive line helped produce the nation's 10th-leading rusher in LeSean McCoy (1,488 yards and 21 touchdowns). Offensive guard C.J. Davis was selected first team All-Big East that year and now is a member of the Carolina Panthers.

Wise's Pitt appointment reunited him with Dave Wannstedt, who he coached with on six prior occasions, and returned him to a place where he received one of his first college coaching positions.

Wannstedt and Wise first worked together on Jackie Sherrill's Pitt coaching staff during the 1977 and 1978 seasons. Wannstedt coached receivers and special teams under Sherrill, while Wise was the Panthers' assistant offensive line coach. They would go on to serve on the same staffs with Oklahoma State, the University of Miami, the Dallas Cowboys and during Wannstedt's head coaching tenures with the Chicago Bears and Miami Dolphins.

Prior to his 2008 return to Pitt, Wise spent 18 years coaching offensive lines in the National Football League, including the 2006 and 2007 seasons with the New York Jets. From 2001 to 2004, he spent four seasons at Miami, where his offensive lines helped produce the two highest individual single-season rushing totals in franchise history. During the 2002 season, the Dolphins rushed for 156.4 yards per game to rank first in the AFC and second in the NFL.

From 1999 to 2000, Wise served with the Carolina Panthers. During the 1999 season, Carolina averaged 4.3 yards per rush to rank fifth in the NFL. Wise served on Wannstedt's Chicago staff from 1993 to 1998. In four of those six seasons, the Bears ranked in the top 10 of the NFL in fewest sacks allowed, including a league-low 15 in 1995. Wise added the duties of assistant head coach his final four seasons in Chicago.

Wise's NFL career began in 1989 with the Dallas Cowboys, where he coached the offensive line for four seasons (1989-1992) under Jimmy Johnson. Wise's line paved the way for Emmitt Smith, who claimed back-to-back NFL rushing titles in 1991 and 1992. Smith rushed for 1,563 yards during the 1991 campaign and 1,713 during the Cowboys' Super Bowl championship season in 1992.

Dallas rolled past Buffalo, 52-17, in Super Bowl XXVII, the Cowboys' first NFL title in 15 years. Wise's offensive front was vital to the championship run, allowing the second-fewest sacks in the NFL (23). He coached a pair of 1992 Pro Bowlers in center Mark Stepnoski, a former Pitt standout, and guard Nate Newton.

Wise also served under Johnson while with the Miami Hurricanes from 1985 to 1988. His UM tenure witnessed the Hurricanes' emergence as a national power. Miami went 34-2 during Wise's final three seasons there, including a 12-0 mark in winning the 1987 national championship.

A native of Newtonville, New York, Wise was an offensive lineman at Ithaca College from 1969 to 1972. He also lettered in lacrosse at Ithaca and played on the school's hockey team. Wise began his coaching career in 1973 at Albany State, where he worked with the outside linebackers. He later coached the offensive lines at Bridgeport (1974), Central Connecticut (1975), and on Jackie Sherrill's staff at Washington State (in 1976 as assistant offensive line coach). Wise's additional collegiate stops include Oklahoma State (under Jimmy Johnson from 1979 to 1983) and Syracuse (1984).

Bob Wylie

THE COUNTER PLAY FROM TWO- AND THREE-TIGHT-END SETS

NFL Alumni

When I was with the Jets, we ran the Wham play. Dante Scarnecchia does a great job in his lecture on the wham series. I am going to add one thing to the wham with two and three tight end schemes.

First, I want to look at the formation utilizing three tight ends (Diagram #1). We have the Y end on the line of scrimmage on the right side. We have another tight end in the wing position on the right side. We have a third tight end in a wing or slot position on the left side. We have a split end to the outside on the left side.

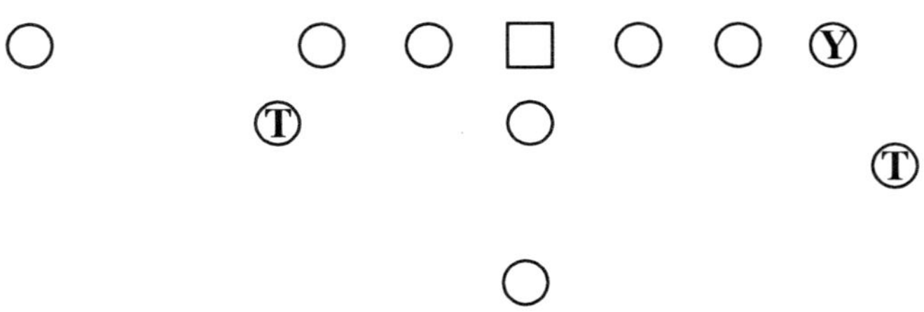

Diagram #1. Three Tight Ends Set

You may use a fullback in one of those two positions with the ends off the line of scrimmage, if the back is used to blocking and running plays from that formation.

If you have been running the wham play as Dante said in his lecture, we did the same blocking. It is Dan Henning's blocking scheme that we all used on the wham.

What we did, when I got to Tampa as the offensive line coach, was to run the inside zone play. We can put the end that is off the line of scrimmage in motion, or move him to any position you want (Diagram #2). We told the tackle and end on the right side to tighten their landmarks down. The reason we did that was because the defense does not stretch as much. So we tightened the landmarks of the defenders we were blocking on the play. The frontside guard, tackle, and end are running the inside zone play and block accordingly.

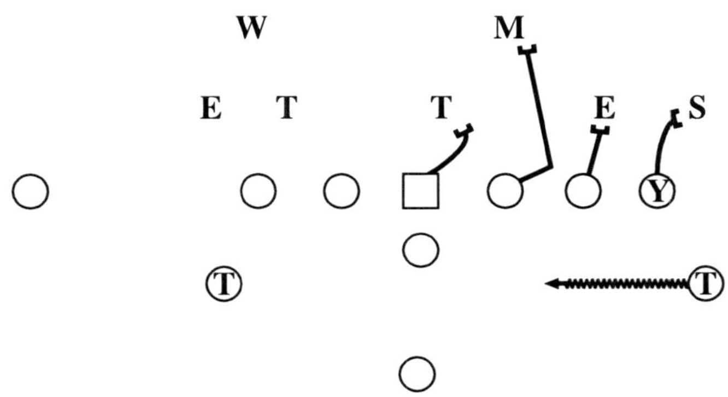

Diagram #2. Blocking: Inside Zone Play

When the motion man disappeared, and the wham block disappeared inside, the defense would not stretch as much. That is the reason we asked the blockers to tighten their landmarks down.

We split our backside guard six inches wider when we were going to run the play over his area. In the course of the game, we were running the wham at the nose tackle (Diagram #3). We run the play at him over and over. As Dante said, if you attack him too many times, the nose tackle will come across the line of scrimmage and attack the wham blocker. He goes after the man that has been blocking him, and he attacks the wham blocker.

When we saw that nose tackle attacking our wham blocker, we made a change in the play. If the Will stacked behind the tackle, we made a call and

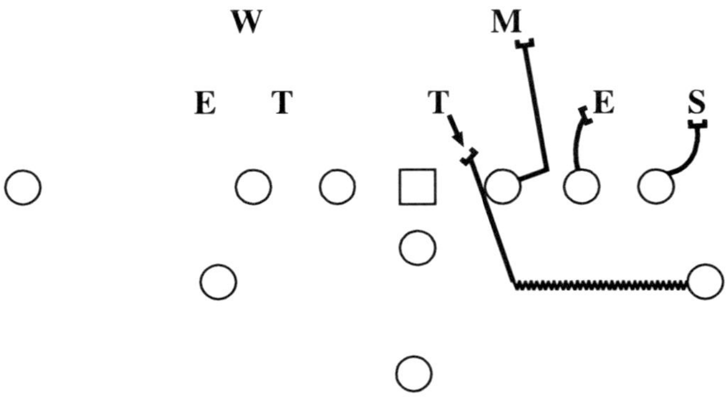

Diagram #3. Wham Block: Nose Tackle

blocked the play on the split end side (Diagram #4), We had the center block the Will linebackers. The guard and tackle blocked the defensive tackle and end. We had the third tight end setting in the wing in a stationary position on the split end side. We wham blocked the nose tackle from the opposite side of the formation. The motion back continued up the field if the tackle was out of the play. He sealed on the Will linebacker if he got through the line.

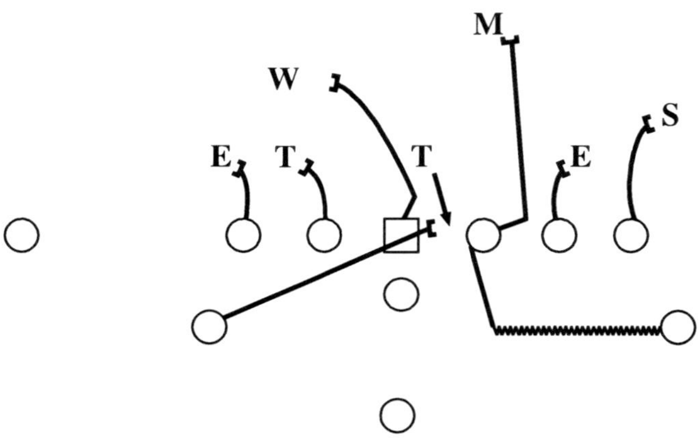

Diagram #4. Wham Block Opposite Side

We made the nose tackle look for the wham block from the right side, but we were blocking him from our left side tight end lined up in the wing set.

The fullback would start tight at the inside leg of the right guard, and then break behind the center (Diagram #5). With the nose tackle attacking the motion back, he took himself out of the play. It left a giant hole in the center of the formation.

If you are going to run the wham play from the right side tight end, this is something you can add to the series.

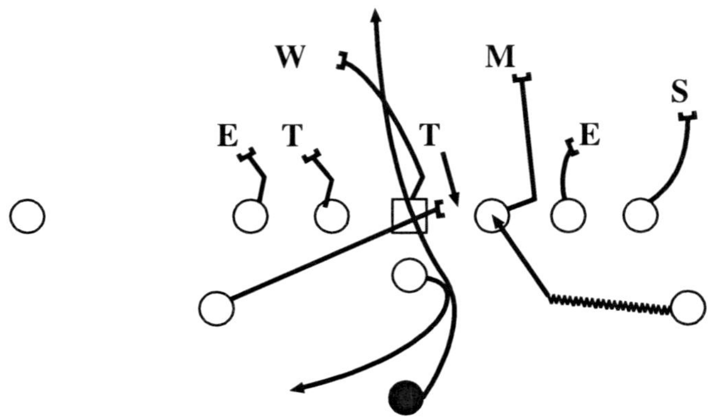

Diagram #5. Fullback With Wham Blocking

I can remember when I was sitting in my office and Sam Wyche came in and said, "You have a call from Joe Gibbs." I picked up the phone and said, "Who is this?" The reply was, "This is Joe Gibbs!" I covered the phone and said, "Oh, crap!" He wanted to know how we blocked the wham play.

When Joe was the coach at Washington, he liked to run these type plays. We had run a similar play against the New Orleans Saints that worked out pretty good. So this is something your can add to the wham package for your offense. This was a neat deal for our offense.

We ran the wham from different formations. We always watch the wham block. We ran the play with an extra tight end, with a fullback at the wing position, and we ran it with motion with the third tight end. Again, we keep our eye on the wham block. When we found the nose tackle attacking our wham motion man, that is when we ran the wham block from the opposite side of the formation.

Each year, I try to give the attendees something to help their offense. Last year, we talked about the duo play. That was our play with two double-teams on a play. We talked about our twin play off the duo play. We only ran the play one way. We ran the bubble to the over defense. When we faced a 1 technique, we wanted to run the twin play, and anytime we had a bubble, we ran the duo play.

If you can take one concept from this clinic, this is the play. You should look at this play. It is a fun play to run. I do not have the fancy slides that most coaches have today. I am in the same situation as Dante is when it comes to the technical equipment used in coaching today.

I was at a high school the other day, and they had a "Chalk Talk" session where they only had a chalkboard with the chalk and eraser. I felt great using the chalkboard. I had chalk dust all over me, but I enjoyed that experience.

Everyone has some type of counter play they like to run. We added an extra tight end to our counter play. We had two tight ends and two backs in the game. It is more of a four-minute deal, but you can run the play on the first down because it is a good play. We call the play 26 counter boss.

We add the extra tight end to the formation. We bring the extra tight end back in motion. He motions across the formation to a spot where our fullback would line up in a weak set. Then we are going to run the play by double-teaming the defensive end. The tackle comes off the block on the end and goes up to the offside linebacker (Diagram #6). There is nothing fancy with the double-team block. We are trying to dent the defense at that point. The tackle has the Mike linebacker if he runs through the B gap.

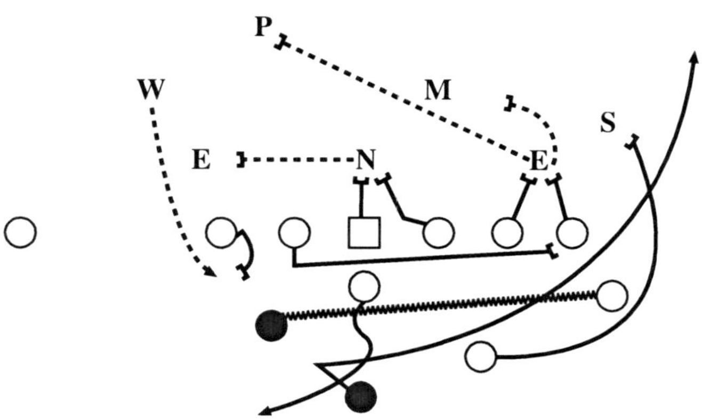

Diagram #6. Double-Team Block to Will Linebacker

The critical thing on double-team blocking is this: the hits and line of force cannot cross. If there is one thing, however, it is this: once you get the blockers into that configuration, it is of the utmost importance that they keep the line of force going parallel.

If you are double-teaming a defender, however you get their footwork in getting to the block, you want their line of force parallel to each other (Diagram #7). You want them hip-to-hip, and working with the footwork, however they can get it done.

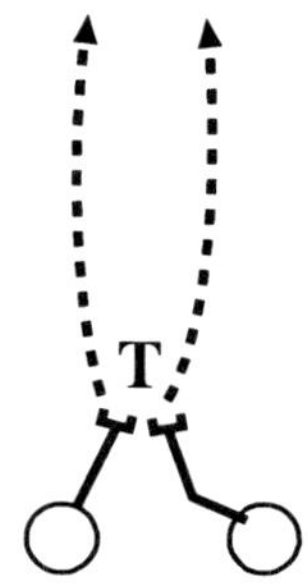

Diagram #7. Double-Team Block

If one of those lines crosses with the other you will not be successful on the block. That is a key point in the double-team block. Their line of force is not cancelling each other out. It is going parallel to each other.

On the counter play the onside tackle has the B gap. He has anyone coming into the B gap, including the linebackers or nose tackle sliding off the center to the B gap. We call the offside linebacker the peg linebacker.

The right guard and center double-team the nose man. The backside guard pulls into the line of scrimmage and comes outside and logs the defender, only if he logs himself.

Following is the key point to all of this. This is something you can take away from this lecture. The pulling guard and the fullback take the Sam and they want to put him into a conflict of assignment (Diagram #8). We always talk about conflict of assignment. "Put the defender in a conflict of interest."

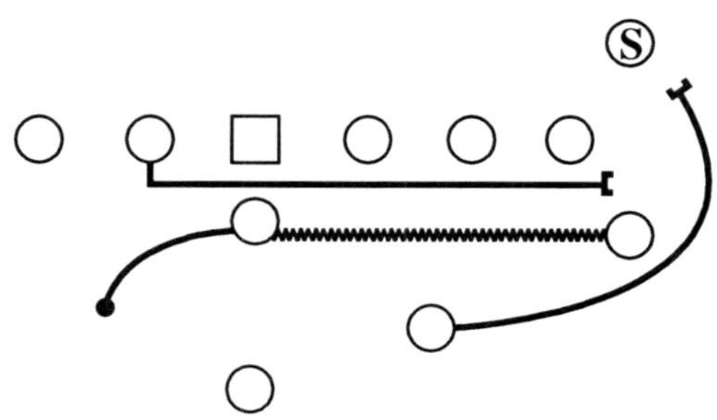

Diagram #8. Conflict of Assignment

The Sam linebacker sees the pulling guard coming at him. Also, he sees the fullback attacking his outside shoulder. The Sam linebacker is thinking, "I can't get outflanked by the fullback. Should I take on the guard or the fullback? What am I going to do?"

We say that Sam linebacker gets into a "conflict of assignment." That is what we are looking for.

The second "puller" is the extra tight end, or Z-end (Diagram #9). The Z-end motions over, and when the ball is snapped, he becomes the second puller.

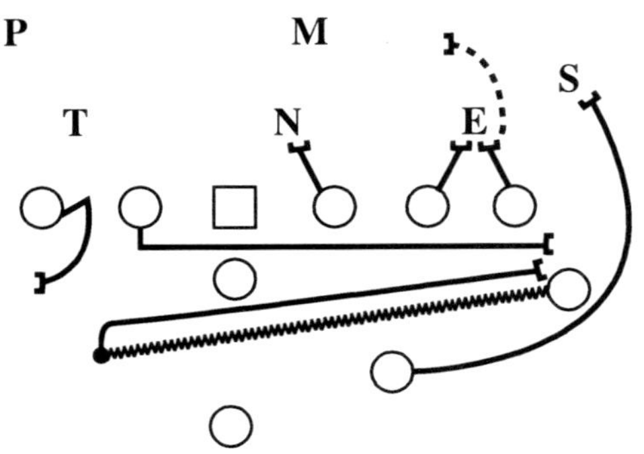

Diagram #9. Extra Puller: Z-End

We tell the pulling guard to only log the Sam linebacker if he logs himself. We tell the extra tight end to pull and to stay close to the double-team block and to block the first defender he sees. We stress for him to always look back from where he came. The Sam linebacker or peg linebacker could run through the gaps. That was the concept of the counter play.

There are a couple of things you can do with this play against a stacked defense. If we face a 9-technique defender, we can make a kick call. If you call "kick," you are going to leave two to the pullers. You can keep the same concept with the fullback attacking the outside edge of the last man on the line of scrimmage, which is the end. You are putting the defensive end into a conflict of assignment because he sees the pulling guard and the fullback. The tight end can release through to the next level.

If you do not make the kick call, the tight end base blocks the 9 technique. If we get a stalemate, we are happy. Then, the guard pulls through and blocks the Sam linebacker. The second puller comes through to the Mike linebacker. The fullback takes the outside and looks for the force defender.

When we put the extra tight end in motion, someone in the secondary has to rotate or move over in the direction of the motion (Diagram #10). You may end up getting an extra blocker to the playside.

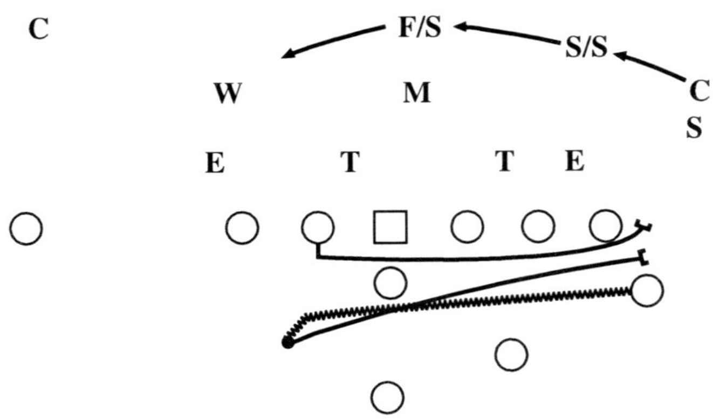

Diagram #10. Motion: Defensive Rotation

Against the 4-3 or even defense we double-team the 3 technique and the tight end has to block the defensive end solo. If we call duo, that means the end has no help on the play and he must block the end by himself.

Again, we are going to put the conflict of assignment on the Sam linebacker with the pulling guard and fullback.

Against a defense that has our three inside people covered that included the two guards and center, we can make a kick call and let the end go through and block down on the other defenders (Diagram #11).

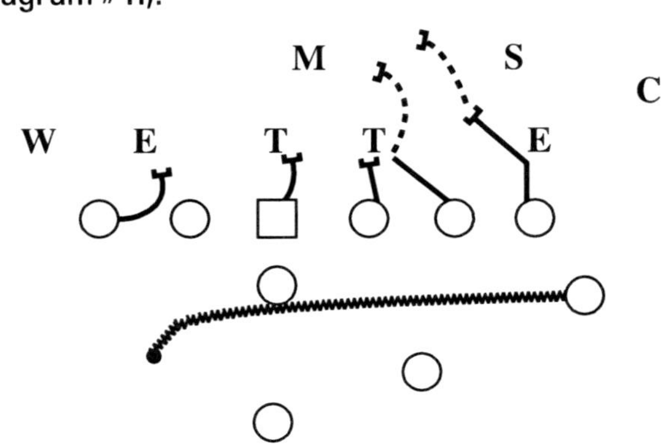

Diagram #11. Kick Call: End Through

You can call deuce, and if you can, cut the backside end, depending how that Will linebacker is playing. It is two different schemes. But if you want to maintain the same scheme, you make the kick call and let the tight end go through and block on the second level. If we do not make the kick call, then the tight end bases up and blocks the defensive end without any help.

You can block everyone down or double-team the 3 technique. If you double-team the 3 technique, the backside A gap is unprotected. If a linebacker ran through the A gap, no one would hit him. For those of you that study film, you can figure out what you want to do on the play.

To carry the play one step further was a neat deal for me. I am talking about running the play on the goal line versus a 6-2-3 defense. We put the Z-tight end on the left side. This would be weak right, close right for us. The tight end gets close on the backside. Now we are forcing the defense to put their adjuster on the wing side to the left. In this instance, the adjuster is the strong safety.

We are going to double-team back with the tight end and tackle. The tackle comes off to the far side linebacker. The guard blocks down on the 1 technique (Diagram #12). The center blocks the 1 technique to his left. We pull the offside guard, and he is looking for the linebacker on the outside. When we get on the goal line, we call these second-level defenders "linebackers." We have the Sam on the wing side, Mike is over our left guard, Will is over our right guard, and the extra linebacker is outside of the tight end.

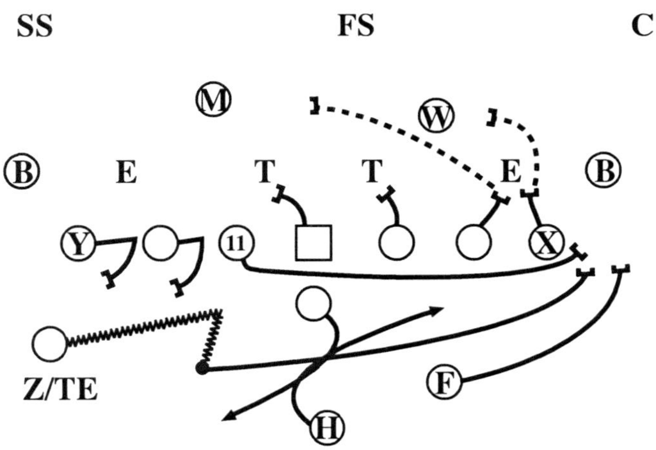

Diagram #12. Vs. 6-2 Goal Line Defense

We still are going to put the extra linebacker in a conflict of assignment situation with our fullback and our pulling guard. The Z-tight end runs the motions toward the quarterback. Then, he returns to the normal set position. This keeps the adjuster on his side of the formation.

Now, we are going to run the play. We can get everyone blocked on this play. We double-team with the backside tackle and Y-tight end. That was one of our goal line plays used against that 6-2 defense. Once we had everyone blocked, we knew we could run other plays against that defense.

I will show you a couple of clips on the play later. The thing I want you to get from all of this is to put the outside defender in a conflict of assignment on the play. You can put the extra tight end in motion to any position you want. You can be creative with this player.

I was talking to a college coach last night. He told me he had a great recruit. If you sign the best players, you become better coaches. If you draft the right players, you can become a really good coach.

In watching the film, let me tell you one thing. If the fullback goes the wrong way, as he did in this case, the play may not work. That may cause a problem for you. We have good plays on film, and we have some bad plays on film.

What I have covered today is something you can add to your two and three tight end offensive package. You can add the counter play (which we call the counter boss package). You can use any names you want for the plays.

ABOUT THE AUTHOR

Bob Wylie was named offensive line coach in the spring of 2014 for the Winnipeg Blue Bombers. Coach Wylie has had tremendous success in the Canadian Football League, and welcomed the challenge of going back to professional football. Prior to his new appointment, Coach Wylie served as offensive line coach under head coach Hue Jackson for the Oakland Raiders.

Wylie, who has more than 30 years of coaching experience, was named the Oakland Raiders offensive line coach on February 1, 2011. During his first year with the Raiders, the offensive line improved from 29th in the NFL in 2010 to fourth in 2011 in total sacks allowed and seventh in sacks per pass play. The line also improved in rushing yards, from 3.1 yards on first down to 4.9 yards and had the leading rusher after the first six games in running back Darren McFadden. The Raiders finished the season ranked seventh in total rushing yards, second in number of 20+ yard rushing plays, and tied for third in rushing plays of over 40 yards.

The offensive line received the Madden Protectors Award in week 6 for their performance against the Cleveland Browns, and rookie guard Stefen Wisniewski was named to the PFW All-Rookie Team. They also paved the way for running back Michael Bush to rush for 977 yards and seven touchdowns.

Prior to his position with the Raiders, Wylie was the offensive line coach for the Denver Broncos (2010). With the Broncos, the offensive line ranked sixth in the NFL, averaging 4.7 yards per carry, during the second half of the season. The club's second-half rushing yards per game improvement of 58.6 yards per game ranked second in the league.

Wylie joined the Broncos after working as an offensive line coach in the Canadian Football League with Saskatchewan (2009) and Winnipeg (2007–2008). Wylie holds the unique distinction of instructing at five different levels of football. He has coached at the Pop Warner, junior high school, high school, college, and professional levels.

During his three years as an offensive line coach in the Canadian Football League, Wylie was part of two teams that played in the Grey Cup: Saskatchewan (2009) and Winnipeg (2007). Believed to be the only assistant coach in CFL history to appear on two Grey Cup teams within his first three years in the league, Wylie coached players to All-Star appearances at every offensive line position (tackle, guard, and center) in the CFL.

Despite four starters missing significant portions of time, Wylie's offensive line with Saskatchewan in 2009 helped the club rank near the top of several offensive statistical categories en route to winning its first division title in 33 years. His effort with the Roughriders followed two years coaching a Winnipeg offensive line that allowed the fewest sacks in the CFL from 2007 to 2008, leading the league in 2007 and ranking second in 2008 while using 14 different starters over the stretch.

Before coaching the offensive line at Syracuse University from 2005 to 2006, Wylie spent eight consecutive years coaching in the NFL. He instructed the Cardinals' offensive line in 2004, with his unit blocking for the NFL's all-time leading rusher, Emmitt Smith, during his final pro season. From 1999 to 2003, Wylie coached the Bears offensive line and helped the club allow an NFL-low 17 sacks in 2001 that propelled the team to an NFC Central title. Bears center Olin Kreutz earned three consecutive Pro Bowl selections (2001–2003) under Wylie while tackle James Williams was named to his first Pro Bowl of his career in 2001.

Wylie's offensive line also helped Chicago running back Anthony Thomas to earn Associated Press NFL Offensive Rookie of the Year honors after he rushed for 1,183 yards in 2001. Thomas's effort marked the seventh time a player totaled at least 1,000 rushing yards in a season with Wylie on staff.

From 1997 to 1998, Wylie was the Bengals tight ends coach and oversaw a group that blocked for running back Corey Dillon, who broke the NFL single-game rushing record, during his consecutive 1,000-yard rushing seasons. He had a one-year stint as the University of Cincinnati's offensive line coach in 1996, a year in which the Bearcats led the Conference USA in rushing and featured four linemen who earned postseason honors, including tackle Jason Fabini. Fabini was one of five players coached by Wylie selected in the NFL Draft.

During four seasons as Tampa Bay's offensive line coach from 1992 to 1995, Wylie's group helped running back Errict Rhett become only the fifth player in NFL history to post consecutive 1,000-yard rushing seasons in his first years in the league (1994–1995). He also coached Pro Football Hall of Fame tackle Anthony Muñoz in training camp in 1993, his final pro season.

Wylie's NFL coaching career began with a two-year stint as the Jets tight ends coach from 1990 to 1991. Before entering the NFL coaching ranks, Wylie coached for 10 seasons at the collegiate level, handling offensive line duties at Brown University (1980–1982), College of the Holy Cross (1983–1984), and Colorado State University (1988–1989) in addition to working as offensive coordinator at Ohio University (1985–1987). At CSU, he worked under NCAA Hall of Fame Coach Earle Bruce.

A native of West Warwick, Rhode Island, Wylie was a teacher and administrator in his hometown from 1973 to 1980. Wylie played linebacker at the college level in Colorado for three years before transferring to Roger Williams College, where he received a bachelor's degree in American Studies. He also earned a master's degree in economics from the University of Rhode Island in 1975.

Inducted into the West Warwick High School Hall of Fame in 1999, Wylie received the NFL's Extra Effort Award in 2001 for his work with Chicago-area youth. He is also one of the organizers of the annual Offensive Line Clinic that takes place in Cincinnati and features some of the nation's top coaches.

A licensed pilot and amateur magician, Wylie was born on February 16, 1951, and he has one daughter (Jennifer) and one grandson (Wylie) as well as a new granddaughter.

WYLIE AT A GLANCE

- Present: Winnipeg Blue Bombers (CFL), Offensive Line
- 2011: Oakland Raiders, Offensive Line
- 2010: Denver Broncos, Assistant Offensive Line
- 2009: Saskatchewan Roughriders (CFL), Offensive Line
- 2007-2008: Winnipeg Blue Bombers (CFL), Offensive Line
- 2005-2006: Syracuse University, Offensive Line
- 2004: Arizona Cardinals, Offensive Line
- 1999-2003: Chicago Bears, Offensive Line
- 1997-1998: Cincinnati Bengals, Tight Ends
- 1996: University of Cincinnati, Offensive Line
- 1992-1995: Tampa Bay Buccaneers, Offensive Line
- 1990-1991: New York Jets, Tight Ends
- 1988-1989: Colorado State University, Offensive Line
- 1985-1987: Ohio University, Offensive Coordinator
- 1983-1984: College of the Holy Cross, Offensive Line
- 1980-1982: Brown University, Offensive Line

About the Editor

Earl Browning is a native of Logan, West Virginia. He currently serves as president of Telecoach, Inc.—an organization that conducts the Nike Coach of the Year Clinics (www.nikecoyfootball.com) and produces the annual *Coach of the Year Clinics Football Manuals* and *Clinic Notes*. A 1958 graduate of Marshall University, he earned his M.Ed. and Rank I education certification from the University of Louisville. From 1958 to 1975, he coached football at various Louisville-area high schools. Among the honors he has been accorded are his appointments to the National Football Foundation and to the College Hall of Fame Advisory Committee on moving the museum to South Bend, Indiana. He was named to the Greater Louisville Football Coaches Association Hall of Legends in 1998. From 1992 to 2010, he served as a radio and television color analyst for Kentucky high school football games, including the Kentucky High School Athletic Association State Championship games. He serves as the Director of Media Relations for the Nike Coach of the Year Football Clinics.